COVERED

GOD'S DESIGN FOR SPIRITUAL PROTECTION

TOM CORNELL

COVERED

GOD'S DESIGN FOR SPIRITUAL PROTECTION

TOM CORNELL

SOZO PUBLISHING

CONTENTS

INTRODUCTION
WHY COVERING MATTERS

'There are moments in every believer's life when the battle intensifies. The air grows thick, the warfare is real, and the pressure mounts beyond what feels survivable. These are not simply moments of temptation or trial, but defining seasons—days of battle that determine direction, destiny, and legacy.

In those moments, many cry out for strength, some fall to their knees in prayer, and others feel abandoned by the very structures that should have supported them. Why is it that some endure the fire and emerge stronger, while others are scorched and scattered by the intensity of the fight?

The answer is often found not in personal gifting or even zeal—but in covering.

Spiritual covering is one of the most misunderstood, neglected, and yet crucial aspects of walking in Kingdom order and authority. Covering is not about hierarchy or control. It is not about submission for the sake of ego or institutionalism.

True covering is about protection, alignment, and empower-ment. It is God's strategy to shield His people from unnecessary wounds, impart generational strength, and ensure that no one walks alone into battle.

We live in a time when spiritual independence is cele-brated. Many believers—particularly in Western contexts—pride themselves on being self-made, self-taught, and self-led. The idea of needing someone over you, walking with you, or covering you feels foreign, even threatening. But this indepen-dent spirit is not a mark of spiritual maturity; it is a symptom of an orphaned heart. And as we will see throughout this book, an orphaned heart is not equipped to win the war that rages in the spirit.

Covering is a Kingdom Pattern

From Genesis to Revelation, God reveals a divine pattern of covering. In the garden, Adam was called to cover Eve—not just in the natural, but in the spiritual. When Adam failed to cover her through leadership and intercession, the door was opened to deception. Later, Noah covered his sons, Abraham covered his household, Moses covered the people, David covered a kingdom, and Jesus, our eternal High Priest, became the ulti-mate covering for mankind.

These were not just roles of leadership—they were func-tions of divine protection.

The tabernacle was covered with animal skins. The ark of the covenant had a mercy seat that covered the law. The blood of sacrifices was a temporary covering for sin. And in the New Covenant, the blood of Jesus not only covers, but cleanses and empowers. At every turn, God has revealed His desire to cover, and His design for us to be covered.

Covering is not optional for the people of God. It is a spiritual necessity.

It is through spiritual covering that sons and daughters are secured, identity is affirmed, anointing is transferred, and protection is provided. In a world of spiritual warfare, deception, false doctrine, and moral collapse, to be uncovered is to be exposed—and exposure brings danger, shame, and defeat.

What Covering Is—And What It's Not

Before we can move forward, we must clear the air of confusion and clarify what covering is not. Spiritual covering is not domination. It is not manipulation. It is not control. These are distortions—abuses of authority that have wounded many in the Body of Christ. The enemy loves to pervert the concept of covering, because he knows how powerful the real thing is.

When leaders abuse their authority, they create resistance to the very structures God intended to bring healing and protection. But the abuse of something never invalidates its proper use. In fact, the enemy only counterfeits what is truly valuable.

Biblical covering is rooted in covenant, not control. It is relational, not institutional. It flows from love, not fear. True covering reflects the heart of the Father. It watches over, intercedes, speaks life, imparts blessing, and carries the burden of responsibility for those under its care. It is not a title but a towel —serving with spiritual strength, maturity, and sacrifice.

Covering is not merely about authority—it is about alignment. And alignment creates access to divine flow.

The War is Real—and So is the Need

We are not living in peacetime. We are in the midst of spiritual war. Ephesians 6 reminds us that we wrestle not against flesh and blood, but against principalities and powers, rulers of darkness, and spiritual wickedness in high places. The war is real—and those without covering often find themselves casualties of conflict they never saw coming.

Spiritual warfare is not fought with physical weapons or emotional resilience alone. It is won through divine strategy, alignment with Kingdom authority, and positioning under protection. When believers are rightly covered, they are not only protected—they are also positioned. Position determines outcome. A soldier out of position becomes a liability. A soldier under command and in alignment becomes a force.

In these last days, spiritual warfare is intensifying. Families are under attack. Marriages are crumbling. Churches are dividing. Leaders are falling. Sons and daughters are drifting. And many are wondering why the fight feels so overwhelming.

Could it be that the Church has lost its covering?
Could it be that leaders have failed to provide true spiritual shelter? Could it be that sons and daughters have rejected authority out of fear or rebellion? Could it be that the orphan spirit has crept into the Church, leaving us exposed in the day of battle?

The answer is yes.

But God is restoring what has been broken. He is calling for a rebuilding of the walls of protection. He is raising up true fathers and mothers in the Spirit. He is aligning houses, churches, and ministries back into Kingdom order. And He is awakening a remnant that longs to walk covered, commissioned, and equipped for the days ahead.

The Cry of the Orphaned Generation

We are witnessing a crisis of covering. The spiritual epidemic of our day is fatherlessness. Not just in the natural— but in the spiritual. Many believers have never known the affirmation of a spiritual father. They've never experienced someone interceding for them, correcting them in love, or guiding them through transition. As a result, they drift, they disconnect, and they isolate.

But every son and daughter longs for covering—even if they don't know how to ask for it.

The orphan spirit causes individuals to distrust authority, reject correction, and run from commitment. It breeds insecurity, comparison, and performance. It cannot receive love, because it fears abandonment. It cannot receive impartation, because it fears manipulation. It cannot receive correction, because it views correction as rejection.

But where the spirit of sonship is embraced, trust is restored, alignment is possible, and covering becomes a blessing.

This book is a call to the orphaned heart. It is a call to return to the Father. It is a call to receive the gift of covering, to seek alignment with spiritual authority, and to become a covering for others as you mature. This is not about dependence. It is about divine design.

Covering is Not Just for the Weak—It's for the Wise

Some believers reject covering because they see it as weakness. But it is not weak to be covered—it is wise. Even Jesus, the Son of God, lived under covering. He said, "I do only what I see my Father doing." He lived in perfect alignment with His Father's will and authority. He submitted to John's baptism. He honored His earthly parents. He obeyed His heavenly Father unto death.

If Jesus lived covered, who are we to live uncovered?

Covering is not a crutch—it is a conduit. It connects us to divine flow. It connects us to generational blessing. It connects us to protection that we cannot create for ourselves. Those who live covered walk in safety, strength, and stability. Those who live uncovered are vulnerable to deception, delay, and destruction.

In the Day of Battle—You Need to Be Covered

There will come a moment in your life when you face an enemy stronger than your last sermon, more cunning than your last fast, and more vicious than your last trial. In that moment, your gifting will not be enough. Your intellect will not be enough. Your charisma will not be enough.

In the day of battle, you need to be covered.
Covered in intercession. Covered in spiritual authority. Covered by the prayers of fathers and mothers in the Spirit.

Covered by a covenant community. Covered in love, truth, and grace.

This book is written to awaken a generation to the power, purpose, and protection of spiritual covering. It will expose the dangers of being uncovered. It will clarify what covering truly is. It will guide you in finding your covering, receiving from your covering, and one day becoming a covering for others.

As you read, may your heart be stirred. May your walls be rebuilt. May your house be aligned. And may your spirit be strengthened to endure the days ahead.

Let's begin the journey—because who covers you could be the difference between victory and defeat.

1

THE PRINCIPLE OF COVERING IN SCRIPTURE

Before we can walk in the benefits of spiritual covering, we must understand its foundation. Covering is not a modern church concept or a denominational idea—it is a divine pattern that has existed since the beginning of time. The principle of covering is woven into the fabric of Scripture, from Genesis to Revelation. It is rooted in the heart of the Father, manifested in the lives of His people, and ultimately fulfilled in Christ.

When we grasp this principle, we begin to see how God has always desired to protect, position, and provide for His people through covering. Without this lens, we risk interpreting authority and alignment through the broken filters of religion, control, or abuse. But with it, we see the wisdom, love, and power of God's design.

Covering in Eden: Adam's Role Over Eve

The very first human relationship was marked by a divine order that included covering. When God created Adam and

Eve, He didn't create them at the same time or in the same way. Adam was formed first from the dust of the ground and received the breath of God. He was given responsibility before Eve ever came on the scene. He was tasked with tending the garden, naming the animals, and stewarding the earth.

Then God said, "It is not good for man to be alone," and He created Eve from Adam's side. This was not a statement of deficiency, but of design. Eve was not an afterthought; she was the completion of Adam. She was formed with intentionality and purpose, not from the ground, but from the side—signifying equality in value, but distinction in role.

Adam's responsibility in that relationship was not to dominate, but to cover. He was to love, protect, instruct, and lead in alignment with the word of God. But when the serpent approached Eve, Adam was silent. The serpent questioned the word of God, and Eve responded. She took of the fruit and ate —and Adam, who was with her (Genesis 3:6), said nothing.

Adam's failure was not simply that he ate the fruit—it was that he failed to cover his wife spiritually. He abdicated his responsibility to stand in the gap, guard the garden, and reinforce the word of the Lord. This act of neglect brought devastating consequences: shame, blame, fear, and separation from God's presence. *In that moment*, the principle of spiritual covering was violated, and the enemy found access.

Yet even in judgment, God revealed His heart to restore covering. He clothed Adam and Eve with animal skins, showing us that even after failure, God will cover what has been exposed. This act pointed forward to the ultimate covering— the Lamb who would be slain to restore what sin had broken.

The Priestly Garments: Covering for the Called

As we move through the Old Testament, we find another powerful picture of covering in the priesthood. When God established the priesthood through Aaron and his sons, He gave specific instructions for the garments they were to wear. These weren't just ceremonial outfits—they were coverings with purpose, each one symbolizing aspects of spiritual authority, holiness, and function.

Exodus 28 details how the high priest's garments included the ephod, breastplate, robe, turban, and sash. These garments were "for glory and for beauty" (Exodus 28:2 KJV), but they also served a deeper function—they signified that the priest was covered by divine authority. Every piece had spiritual meaning, from the names of the tribes engraved on the stones to the bells and pomegranates on the hem of the robe.

The robe in particular had a hem that, when intact, allowed the priest to minister safely in the Holy Place. If the robe was torn or incomplete, the priest risked death. Why? Because you cannot enter God's presence uncovered. Holiness, order, and covering mattered to God.

When the priests were clothed, they were covered for service. They weren't functioning in their own strength or authority—they were moving under God's covering, which allowed them to minister to the people, intercede for the nation, and carry the presence of the Lord.

In fact, the absence of covering was considered nakedness and brought shame. That which is uncovered is vulnerable. But that which is covered by God is protected and positioned to release His glory.

The Covering of the Tabernacle and the Ark

The tabernacle itself was a structure of layers and coverings. Exodus 26 describes how it was to be covered with curtains of fine linen, goat's hair, ram skins dyed red, and hides of sea cows. These layers weren't just practical for weather—they represented spiritual truths.

The outer coverings were plain, even unattractive, but the inner layers were detailed, beautiful, and holy. This teaches us that true covering is often unseen and undervalued by the world, but it carries tremendous spiritual weight. Protection doesn't always look glamorous—but it is essential.

At the center of the tabernacle was the Ark of the Covenant. And what sat on top of the Ark? The Mercy Seat. The lid of the Ark was called a covering. Inside the Ark were the tablets of the law, but over them was the mercy seat, and upon the mercy seat was the blood of atonement. This is profound: *the law was covered by mercy.*

Where there was judgment, God placed a covering. Where there was failure, God provided blood. Where there was exposure, God released grace. Covering, then, is not just about protection from enemies—it is about shielding us from the judgment we deserve, allowing mercy to triumph.

This is the heart of the Father. He has always desired to cover what is broken, to redeem what is lost, and to restore what has been defiled. But He does it through divine patterns, not random acts. And one of the patterns He uses is covering through spiritual authority.

The Covering of Boaz over Ruth

Another striking example of covering is found in the story of Ruth and Boaz. After the loss of her husband and the decision to stay with Naomi, Ruth finds herself gleaning in the field of Boaz—a man of integrity and authority. Naomi instructs Ruth to go to the threshing floor and lay at Boaz's feet. When she does, she makes a bold request:

> *"Spread your covering over me, for you are a kinsman redeemer"*
> *(Ruth 3:9)* NASB

Boaz's garment represented his authority and his ability to cover Ruth not only as a woman, but as a part of the redemptive line of Israel. When Boaz covered her, he was accepting responsibility. He was saying, "I will redeem you. I will protect you. I will provide for you."

This image speaks prophetically of Christ, our Redeemer, who spreads His covering over us and brings us into covenant. But it also reveals how authority, when aligned with righteousness, becomes a safe covering for others. Boaz did not use his authority to control or manipulate Ruth—he used it to redeem her and restore her lineage.

Jesus: Our Ultimate Covering

All throughout Scripture, we see temporary coverings: garments, priesthoods, rituals, and systems. But all of these pointed to one ultimate reality: Jesus Christ is our covering.

He is the fulfillment of every type and shadow. He is the Lamb whose blood covers our sin. He is the High Priest who enters the Most Holy Place on our behalf. He is the Mediator of a better covenant. He is the Shepherd who watches over our soul. He is the King who rules with justice. He is the Bride-groom who clothes His bride with righteousness.

Isaiah 61:10 (NIV) says, *"He has clothed me with garments of salvation and arrayed me in a robe of righteousness."*

When we come under the lordship of Jesus, we are no longer naked and ashamed—we are covered in His grace, right-eousness, and power.

Yet even Jesus, in His earthly ministry, modeled covering. He lived in submission to His Father. He honored spiritual alignment. He functioned as a Son under authority so that we could live as sons and daughters who are covered. His ministry was not rogue, rebellious, or independent—it was in alignment.

The Principle in Practice

So what does this mean for us today? It means that spiritual covering is not a suggestion—it's a pattern we are called to walk in. We are to be covered in Christ, covered by spiritual leader-ship, and in turn, become coverings for others. No believer is called to live isolated, unsubmitted, or independent of spiritual authority.

Covering protects us from deception. It positions us for promotion. It shields us in warfare. It speaks on our behalf when we cannot speak for ourselves. It prays for us when we are too weak to pray. It holds us accountable when we want to drift. And it blesses us when we are ready to be sent.

Every great move of God in Scripture was birthed in align-ment. Every great leader had a covering. Every son and daughter who walked in power was first positioned under authority.

Elijah had a mantle, but Elisha received it only by walking closely and honoring the covering. Moses was a deliverer, but Joshua received impartation through alignment. Paul was an apostle, but Timothy fulfilled his ministry under Paul's spiritual fatherhood.

You cannot receive what you do not honor. And you cannot carry what you are unwilling to be covered by.

Conclusion: Returning to the Pattern

The principle of covering in Scripture is not just theological —it is transformational. It is God's way of protecting, preparing, and promoting His people. In a world full of spiritual chaos, deception, and danger, we must return to the divine pattern.

Covering is not about being controlled—it's about being covered with God's protection. It's about being connected, aligned, and rooted. It's about submitting to spiritual fathers, walking in Kingdom order, and being prepared to become a covering for the next generation.

The Church must restore the value of covering—not as a system of control, but as a strategy of Kingdom strength.

You were never meant to live uncovered.

You were created to walk in covenant. You were called to live aligned. And you were designed to receive from those who have gone before you, so you can release what you carry to those who come after you. Let the Word do its work in your heart. Let the pattern speak. Let the principle become practice.

You were meant to be covered.

Discussion Questions

1 . How does understanding the principle of covering from Genesis (with Adam and Eve) reshape your perspective on spiritual authority and personal responsibility?

2 . In what ways do the garments of the priests and the coverings of the tabernacle illustrate the seriousness and beauty of God's covering in your own life today?

3 . Are there areas in your life where you've resisted or misunderstood spiritual covering? What steps can you take to walk in alignment and trust the protection and provision that comes from being covered?

2

THE NATURE OF AUTHORITY AND ALIGNMENT

S piritual authority is not a man-made concept—it is a divine structure, rooted in the nature of God Himself. From the beginning of creation to the establishment of His Kingdom in the earth, God has always operated through delegated authority and divine alignment.

When we speak of covering, we cannot ignore the foundational truth that covering flows from authority. But authority must be rightly understood—because when it is, it unlocks protection, empowerment, and access to Kingdom order.

Authority that is not understood is often resisted. Authority that is abused creates trauma. But authority that is honored releases alignment, and alignment is the pathway to life, blessing, and overflow.

In this chapter, we will uncover three critical truths:

- What spiritual authority truly is

- The difference between delegated and absolute authority
- How alignment positions us for both protection and empowerment

Understanding Spiritual Authority

Spiritual authority originates from God, not man. He is the source. Every structure of authority in heaven and on earth ultimately finds its legitimacy in Him.

Romans 13:1 says, "There is no authority except from God, and those that exist have been instituted by God." NIV

This passage is not a blanket endorsement of every leader's actions, but it does reveal that order is God's design.

From heaven to earth, from angels to apostles, from families to governments—God ordains authority to govern, protect, and release purpose. Without it, chaos reigns. In the natural world, authority maintains order. In the spiritual world, authority maintains covering.

But many have a distorted view of spiritual authority. Some think it's synonymous with control, superiority, or rank. Others believe authority is earned through gifting or charisma. Still others reject the concept altogether because of wounds caused by abusive leaders. Yet God's definition of authority is different.

In the Kingdom, authority is servanthood empowered by Heaven. Jesus exemplified this. He said in Matthew 20:25–28 that the rulers of the Gentiles "lord it over" others, but it shall not be so among you. Instead, whoever wants to be great must become a servant, and whoever wants to be first must become a slave. This is a shocking redefinition. In God's Kingdom, authority is not the right to dominate—it is the grace to serve under Heaven's commission.

Jesus had all authority, and yet He washed feet. He commanded storms, yet welcomed children. He rebuked devils, but restored the broken. His authority was not loud for attention—it was weighty in the Spirit. Why? Because it was submitted.

True spiritual authority carries weight, not just volume. It carries grace, not just rules. It flows from heavenly commission, not human ambition.

Delegated vs. Absolute Authority

Understanding the difference between delegated and absolute authority is vital in building a healthy theology and practice of spiritual covering. Absolute authority belongs to God alone. He is sovereign, holy, and without fault. His judgments are perfect. His will is just. He answers to no one and needs no counsel. He is the ultimate source of all authority.

Delegated authority, on the other hand, is what God entrusts to individuals in specific roles for specific purposes. This could be spiritual leaders, parents, employers, or even government officials. Delegated authority carries responsibility, but it is always under accountability to God. The danger comes when delegated authority tries to act as if it is absolute.

When a pastor begins to think they are above correction...
When a prophet refuses to be judged by others...
When a father becomes abusive instead of protective...

When a leader uses authority to serve themselves instead of
others...
...that's how authority becomes distorted.

This is how spiritual abuse occurs—not because authority
exists, but because it is used without submission to God's ultimate rule. True authority always stays under authority. A leader
who is not under covering is dangerous, no matter how
anointed they appear.
Even Jesus operated under delegated authority.

He said in John 12:49, "For I have not spoken on My own authority,
but the Father who sent Me has Himself given Me a commandment
—what to say and what to speak." ESV

If the Son of God did not function in His own authority,
how much more should we walk in humble submission to the
One who sends us? Delegated authority is powerful, but only
when it flows from intimacy, obedience, and accountability to
the One who gives it.

This understanding creates both humility and clarity.
When you walk under delegated authority, you are walking
under a divine assignment. You are not trying to create power—
you are simply aligned with power.

Alignment Is Protection

Alignment is not about restriction—it is about protec-
tion.Too many people view submission to spiritual authority as
a limitation. They see covering as a ceiling rather than a shield.
But the truth is, alignment is a spiritual safeguard in a world of
warfare, deception, and temptation.

Consider this: a car that is out of alignment may still move, but it will drift, wobble, and eventually damage itself. It may even crash. In the same way, believers who are not spiritually aligned may still appear active, but over time, they experience internal wear, emotional instability, and relational breakdowns.

When you are aligned under spiritual authority, you are covered in intercession, correction, and spiritual oversight. You are not left alone in the battle. You are not vulnerable to every wind of doctrine. You are not making decisions in isolation. You are walking in the safety of alignment.

Psalm 133 paints a vivid picture of alignment and covering.

It says, "Behold, how good and pleasant it is when brothers dwell in unity! It is like the precious oil on the head, running down on the beard...on the collar of his robes." Psalm 133:1-2 ESV

This passage speaks of alignment—from the head (authority) to the beard (maturity) to the robe (body). Where there is alignment, there is anointing. And where there is anointing, there is life and blessing forevermore.

Alignment creates a flow.
Misalignment creates a blockage.

You may have gifting, but if you're out of alignment, that gifting becomes disconnected from divine supply. You may have passion, but without alignment, that passion can turn into rebellion. You may have revelation, but out of alignment, it breeds pride instead of transformation.

Submission and alignment are not just relational—they are positional. When you are under the right covering, Heaven backs you. You are not building on your own foundation—you are standing on a grace that goes before you and covers you behind.

Alignment Is Empowerment

Not only does alignment bring protection—it also releases empowerment. There is a spiritual principle at work here: what you are under, you can receive from. What you honor, you can access. What you align with, you can be empowered by.

We see this throughout Scripture:

- Moses and Joshua — Joshua was not chosen because of charisma, but because of alignment. He served Moses, followed him closely, and honored his covering. As a result, Moses laid hands on him and imparted wisdom and authority.
- Elijah and Elisha — Elisha refused to leave Elijah's side. His alignment brought him into a double portion. He didn't ask for a mantle—he inherited it through loyalty, submission, and service.
- Jesus and the Centurion — The Roman centurion in Matthew 8 said, "I too am a man under authority, with soldiers under me." He understood that Jesus' power came not from being independent, but from being under divine authority. And because of that faith, Jesus healed his servant with just a word.

These examples show us that alignment opens the door to power, favor, and inheritance.

Many people today are striving for influence, begging for doors to open, or praying for supernatural increase. But they neglect the principle of alignment. They want the mantle without the submission. They want the blessing without the burden. They want the influence without the intimacy that comes from being under a covering.

But God does not release lasting empowerment to those who are disconnected. Empowerment flows through alignment, not around it.

Signs You Are Out of Alignment

To walk in alignment, we must also recognize when we're not. Here are some signs that a person may be out of spiritual alignment:

- Chronic isolation — They refuse spiritual accountability or relationship with authority.
- Resentment toward correction — They bristle when challenged or confronted.
- Spiritual burnout — They are operating in their own strength with no replenishing flow.
- Restlessness and instability — They move frequently from place to place, church to church, covering to covering.
- Pride and self-promotion — They desire position or platform more than submission and growth.

Alignment requires humility. It is not about dependence, but about honor. It is not about losing your voice—it is about stewarding your voice under authority so it carries weight in the Spirit.

How to Return to Alignment

If you find yourself out of alignment, there is good news:

God's grace is sufficient, and He is always calling His sons and daughters back into position. Here are steps to returning to alignment:

1. Repent for rebellion or independence — Ask the Lord to forgive any pride, bitterness, or distrust that has kept you from honoring authority.
2. Pray for discernment — Seek the Holy Spirit's guidance in identifying the right spiritual leaders or coverings in your life.
3. Initiate accountability — Don't wait to be chased down. Humble yourself, reach out, and express your desire to walk in alignment.
4. Honor your covering — This doesn't mean blind obedience, but it does mean respect, teachability, and trust.
5. Stay consistent — Alignment is not a one-time event. It's a posture of the heart and a lifestyle of honor.

Conclusion: Walking in the Blessing of Alignment

Authority and alignment are not outdated religious concepts—they are timeless Kingdom principles that bring strength, safety, and supernatural empowerment. When you understand the nature of spiritual authority, you begin to value the coverings God places in your life.

You stop seeing them as ceilings and begin seeing them as shields. You no longer view alignment as a limitation but as a lifeline. You walk with confidence, knowing you are not alone, not exposed, and not unauthorized.

Covering flows from authority, and authority only carries

weight when it is aligned with Heaven. As you position yourself under God's order—submitted, aligned, and rightly connected —you will find not only protection in the day of battle, but purpose in your assignment and power to fulfill it.

Don't despise authority. Don't resist alignment. Learn to love the safety of covering, the beauty of spiritual order, and the empowerment that flows when you walk in the grace of divine alignment.

Discussion Questions

1. In what ways have you seen spiritual authority misunderstood or misused, either personally or in church culture? How did that impact your view of leadership or submission?

2. How does Jesus' model of authority challenge the way we typically view leadership roles today? What does it practically look like to lead as a servant under God's authority?

3. What areas of your life may need realignment with God's spiritual order? What practical steps can you take this week to position yourself under healthy covering or accountability?

3
___

FATHERS, SHEPHERDS, AND
COVERINGS

C overing is not just a principle. It's not merely a theological concept or a mystical transaction in the spirit. Covering is relational. It is carried by people. It is embodied by men and women God raises to be spiritual fathers, shepherds, mentors, and apostolic leaders. God doesn't cover His people with titles or systems—He covers them with people.

In a world where institutional hierarchy has often replaced relational connection, the Church must recover the original heart of spiritual covering: fatherhood and shepherding. Titles alone do not cover. Systems alone do not nurture. It takes people—anointed, appointed, mature leaders—who understand the heart of God and carry His burden to cover others in love, truth, and spiritual oversight.

In this chapter, we will explore:

- What spiritual fathers do

- The roles of pastors, mentors, and apostles in the covering relationship
- The spiritual weight and responsibility of being a covering

What Spiritual Fathers Do

Spiritual fathers are more than teachers, more than leaders, and more than friends. They are carriers of identity, inheritance, and insight. Paul said it clearly in 1 Corinthians 4:15, "Though you have countless guides in Christ, you do not have many fathers. For I became your father in Christ Jesus through the gospel."

That statement exposes a painful truth: there are many instructors, but few fathers. Many can teach you doctrine, but not many will father you through development. Many can correct you, but not many will cover you. Spiritual fathers are rare, not because they're inaccessible, but because they are often unrecognized or rejected in a culture that idolizes independence and performance.

Spiritual Fathers Impart Identity

When Jesus was baptized, the heavens opened, the Spirit descended like a dove, and the Father's voice thundered: "This is My beloved Son, in whom I am well pleased" (Matthew 3:17). Before Jesus did a single miracle, cast out one demon, or preached to a crowd, He received identity and affirmation from His Father.

Every son or daughter needs to hear, "You are mine. You are loved. I am pleased with you." This is what fathers do. They settle the issue of identity in the heart of the believer. They silence the need to perform. They break off shame. They give names. They call destiny forth.

Spiritual fathers are not threatened by your gift. They help you discover it and steward it. They don't compete with sons— they cover them.

Spiritual Fathers Provide Correction and Comfort

A true father disciplines, but not out of anger. Hebrews 12 tells us that those who are loved by the Father are also corrected by Him. Fathers correct not to control, but to protect. They see what a son may not yet see. They warn, instruct, and even rebuke, but always with a heart to restore.

They are not harsh—they are firm in love. Correction without comfort leads to rebellion. Comfort without correction leads to entitlement. But spiritual fathers walk in both. They are present in failure. They are a voice of truth in confusion. They don't abandon their sons when they fall—they intercede and restore.

Spiritual Fathers Intercede and War for Their Sons

A true covering is not passive. It is not about status—it is about intercession. Fathers stand in the gap for their sons and daughters. They war in prayer. They fast. They weep. They carry the burden of those they cover as if it were their own.

Moses interceded for Israel when God was ready to judge them. Paul travailed in prayer for the Galatians until Christ was formed in them. Elijah laid his body over a dead boy until life returned to him. Fathers do not simply instruct from a distance —they contend in the Spirit until breakthrough comes.

Pastors, Mentors, and Apostles in Covering

While all spiritual fathers may not carry the title "pastor" or "apostle," many pastors and apostles are called to be spiritual coverings. Understanding the different roles they play helps us better identify how God positions leaders for our protection and development.

Pastors: Shepherds Who Cover the Flock

The word "pastor" in Scripture literally means shepherd. A shepherd feeds, leads, protects, and watches over the flock. Jesus described Himself as the Good Shepherd who lays down His life for the sheep (John 10:11). In the same way, spiritual pastors are not hirelings—they do not run when wolves come. They stand between danger and their people. They feed sound doctrine. They protect from error. They weep with the broken.

A true pastor knows the flock. They are not CEO figures, removed from the lives of the people. They are present, accessible, and full of compassion. And most importantly, they are submitted to Christ, the Chief Shepherd.

Pastors are often the first layer of spiritual covering in the local church. They may not be apostles or spiritual fathers in a formal sense, but they function as shepherds who guard the gates and watch for the souls of those entrusted to their care (Hebrews 13:17).

Mentors: Coaches Who Guide Development

Mentors play a unique and valuable role in spiritual growth. Unlike fathers, who deal with identity and legacy, mentors often focus on development and assignment. They help you mature in character, giftings, and ministry expression.

Mentors provide wisdom, share experience, and offer guidance for navigating seasons and decisions. They may not carry the weight of fatherhood, but they complement the role of fathers by sharpening and equipping. However, a mentor alone is not a covering. You can be coached without being covered. The difference is relational depth, covenant, and spiritual authority. Mentors help refine, but fathers build and protect.

Apostles: Builders and Gatekeepers

The apostolic role carries a unique grace for governing, building, and covering. Apostles are not simply church planters or traveling preachers. In biblical terms, apostles establish foundations, raise leaders, and oversee spiritual structures.

Paul functioned as a father and apostle. He planted churches, ordained leaders, dealt with doctrinal issues, corrected sin, and interceded for his spiritual sons. His letters were not just teachings—they were fatherly epistles of correction, comfort, and commissioning.

Apostles carry a regional and generational grace. They don't just cover individuals—they cover houses, movements, and territories. They are spiritual architects who lay foundations and watch over the structural integrity of the church.

When apostles function rightly, they are not authoritarian —they are fathers who build. They don't hoard authority— they release and empower.

The Weight of Covering Others

Being a covering is not glamorous—it is grueling. It requires spiritual maturity, emotional health, and a deep relationship with God. Many want influence, but few want responsibility. Many want a following, but few want the weight of fatherhood.

Here are just a few dimensions of that weight:

Spiritual Burden
Covering someone means you carry them in the Spirit. You discern their battles. You carry the weight of their calling. You groan in prayer when they are drifting. You feel responsibility even when you are not to blame.

Paul said, "Who is weak, and I am not weak? Who is made to stumble, and I do not burn with indignation?" (2 Corinthians 11:29). This is the cry of a true covering: when my sons are hurting, I feel it. When they fall, I weep. When they rise, I rejoice.

Relational Risk
Fathers who cover risk being misunderstood, rejected, and even betrayed. Covering is not always honored. Sons sometimes walk away. Some bite the hand that fed them. Some misuse access or dishonor the grace they received.

Jesus had twelve, but one betrayed Him. Paul poured into Demas, who later abandoned him. Elijah fathered Elisha, but Gehazi later walked in greed. Covering always carries the risk of heartbreak—but love takes the risk anyway.

True fathers love without guarantee. They do not cover

for applause—they cover because they carry the Father's heart.

Covenantal Commitment

Covering is not seasonal—it is covenantal. You don't stop being a father because your son moves cities. You don't stop covering someone because they make a mistake. You don't disconnect because of disagreement.

Of course, not every relationship is permanent. There are healthy transitions. But true coverings don't abandon—they bless, release, and remain available. Covenant doesn't mean control—it means commitment. It means, "Even if you fall, I will pray. Even if you leave, I will bless. Even if I am grieved, I will remain fatherly."

What Coverings Are Not

As important as it is to understand the role of coverings, it is just as vital to recognize what coverings are not. Misunderstanding leads to manipulation or abuse. Let's set the record straight.

- Coverings are not dictators.
- Coverings are not controllers of decisions.
- Coverings are not infallible or all-knowing.
- Coverings are not owners.

Coverings do not replace the Holy Spirit. They do not dictate personal choices. They do not override conscience. They walk with you, they pray for you, they counsel you, and when needed, they correct you in love. But they do not control your life.

Spiritual covering is not about diminishing your voice—it is about strengthening your walk.

Recognizing and Honoring the Coverings in Your Life

One of the most important steps a believer can take is to recognize who God has placed as a spiritual covering in their life. Sometimes that person may not have a formal title. Sometimes they may not look impressive. But they carry a grace to speak into your life, walk with you through the process, and guard you in prayer and truth.

Ask yourself:

- Who speaks truth to me even when it's uncomfortable?
- Who is praying for me regularly?
- Who sees my potential and still speaks to my character?
- Who has been there when I've failed, not just when I succeeded?

That person is likely your covering. Honor them. Receive from them. Submit to them in the Lord. Don't take them for granted. Don't become familiar. Honor creates access. Familiarity breeds offense.

Conclusion: The Restoration of Spiritual Fathers

We are living in a time where God is restoring the ministry of fathers in the Church. The spirit of Elijah is being poured out again—not in fiery sermons alone, but in fatherly coverings. Malachi 4:6 says, "He will turn the hearts of the fathers to the children, and the hearts of the children to their fathers."

This is not just about natural family—this is about spiritual alignment. The curse is broken when coverings are restored. Identity is healed. Power is released. Legacy is preserved. Let us be a people who honor spiritual fathers. Let us also prepare to become coverings as we mature. The next generation needs more than instructors—they need fathers, shepherds, and coverings.

The war is too intense, the deception too deep, and the calling too high for sons and daughters to walk uncovered. May the Spirit of God raise up coverings in every city, in every church, and in every nation—leaders who love well, lead wisely, and cover faithfully.

Discussion Questions

1 Why do you think spiritual fatherhood is so rare in today's church culture, even though the need is clearly great?

2 Which role—pastor, mentor, or apostle—has played the most significant part in your own spiritual journey so far, and how did that relationship impact your growth?

3 Covering involves emotional risk, spiritual burden, and covenantal commitment. What might be holding you back from stepping into this role for someone else—or from receiving it from someone in your life?

4

WHAT A COVERING PROVIDES

Spiritual covering is not merely a theological idea or a symbolic gesture. It is a real, tangible, spiritual reality that carries practical and supernatural benefits. Just as an umbrella protects from the rain and armor shields in battle, a spiritual covering provides what no individual can fully provide for themselves—protection, purpose, correction, encouragement, impartation, and inheritance.

Many believers walk through life spiritually exposed, vulnerable to attack, confused about their identity, and weary from carrying burdens they were never meant to carry alone. This is not God's design. Covering is a provision of the Father's heart—meant to establish us, secure us, and propel us into our destiny.

In this chapter, we will unpack five major provisions of spiritual covering:

- Protection from demonic attack
- Clarity of identity and purpose

- Correction and encouragement
- Impartation of grace and wisdom
- Access to spiritual inheritance

1. Protection from Demonic Attack

Perhaps the most urgent function of spiritual covering is protection. The spiritual realm is not neutral. It is a battlefield. Whether we are aware of it or not, we are constantly surrounded by invisible opposition—principalities, powers, rulers of darkness, and spiritual wickedness in high places (Ephesians 6:12). To be uncovered is to be vulnerable. To be covered is to be shielded.

When a believer is under spiritual covering, they are not alone in the fight. Their covering stands between them and the attack, just as a shepherd stands between the sheep and the wolf.

In Ezekiel 22:30 (NIV), God says, "I looked for someone among them who would build up the wall and stand before me in the gap on behalf of the land..."

That is what a covering does—it stands in the gap. When Satan sought to sift Peter like wheat, Jesus declared, "But I have prayed for you" (Luke 22:32). This is the language of covering—standing, shielding, praying, protecting.

Spiritual attacks often begin in subtle ways—discouragement, confusion, compromise. But when someone is covered, the enemy's assignments are discerned early, resisted quickly, and broken through prayer and counsel. Coverings do not replace your personal spiritual warfare, but they reinforce it.

Think of Moses on the hill while Joshua fought Amalek. As long as Moses' hands were raised—symbolizing covering and intercession—Joshua prevailed. But when the hands dropped, the enemy advanced. This shows us that spiritual covering can shift the tide of battle.

If the enemy can isolate you, he can devour you. If he can remove your covering, he can wear you out. But when you are properly covered, you are part of a fortified spiritual structure, where you are not easily shaken or overrun.

2. Identity and Purpose

Another key benefit of spiritual covering is clarity in identity and purpose. A true covering does not suppress who you are—it helps you discover who you are in Christ. Identity is not formed in isolation. Sons and daughters need fathers and mothers who speak into their lives, affirm their worth, and call out their God-given assignments. *Without covering,* identity is vulnerable to the voices of culture, comparison, and insecurity. But a covering becomes a voice of truth—a mirror that reflects what heaven sees.

Consider how Jesus called Simon a "rock" long before Peter acted like one. That was covering. Jesus was speaking identity into a man who was still in process. Likewise, Paul spoke to Timothy not just as a co-laborer, but as a "true son in the faith" (1 Timothy 1:2). He affirmed him, reminded him of his gift, and exhorted him to walk in boldness.

Many believers are gifted, but insecure. Anointed, but unsure of their assignment. Their sense of worth is fragile, and their calling feels undefined. But when they come under a healthy covering, they begin to hear consistent affirmation: You are a son. You are chosen. You are called. You are not alone.

Coverings are like spiritual mirrors—they help us see ourselves rightly. They also help refine our purpose. It is not uncommon for someone to have a prophetic promise or a dream but lack the clarity and structure to fulfill it. A spiritual covering provides wisdom, timing, and accountability that positions that dream for fulfillment.

Coverings ask questions like:

- What is God saying about your next season?
- What has He already entrusted you with?
- Are you being faithful with what's in your hand?
- What needs to grow before you're ready for more?

This is how purpose gets shaped and sustained. Not in isolation, but in alignment.

3. Correction and Encouragement

Many people want the encouragement of a covering but resist the correction. Yet both are essential—and both are a sign of love.

Hebrews 12:6 (NIV) reminds us that "the Lord disciplines the one He loves, and He chastens everyone He accepts as His son."

True love does not enable destruction—it interrupts it. A covering is not just a cheerleader. It's a guardian of destiny. It's someone who is willing to confront the cracks in your character before they cause collapse.

Correction is a gift. But when you are uncovered, no one sees the small compromises. No one challenges the drift. No one warns you of the slow fade. But when you're covered, your blind spots are not fatal—they're caught in time.

Correction must always come in the context of relationship. It is not shame-based or harsh—it is restorative and life-giving. As Paul wrote in Galatians 6:1, "If someone is caught in a sin, you who live by the Spirit should restore that person gently."

A true covering is not out to embarrass you. They're out to restore you. And when you're willing to receive correction, you position yourself for fruitfulness without collapse. Equally important is encouragement. Life can be brutal. Ministry can be lonely. Warfare can be exhausting. We all need voices that remind us: Don't quit. You're not disqualified. You're not alone. God is still with you.

Coverings offer that kind of encouragement—not just in a sermon, but in the secret place of intercession, a phone call during your darkest hour, or a prophetic word at just the right moment. Correction keeps you aligned. Encouragement keeps you moving forward. Both come through the channel of spiritual covering.

4. Impartation of Grace and Wisdom

Covering is not just about relationship—it is also about impartation. When you are rightly aligned, you are positioned to receive grace that flows from someone else's walk with God. This is not mystical—it is deeply biblical.

In Romans 1:11, Paul writes, "I long to see you so that I may impart to you some spiritual gift to make you strong." Impartation is the spiritual transmission of grace, wisdom, or anointing from one person to another. And it happens most powerfully in the context of covering.

Consider Elisha. He did not receive Elijah's mantle by accident. He walked with him. Served him. Stayed close. And at the end of Elijah's life, when others watched from a distance, Elisha followed him to the end. Why? Because Elisha was aligned. He was covered. And he received the double portion because he was in position to inherit it.

You can't receive what you dishonor.
You can't carry what you're unwilling to walk under.

Spiritual coverings are often carriers of grace, wisdom, and anointing you need—but not through osmosis. You must stay close, serve, listen, honor, and receive. Coverings may not always "lay hands" to impart something dramatic, but their very life becomes a well from which you draw. Their stories become your wisdom. Their victories become your blueprint. Their failures become your warning signs.

Some things are taught.
Others are caught.
And you only catch them when you walk in covering.

5. Access to Spiritual Inheritance

One of the most beautiful functions of spiritual covering is the transfer of inheritance. Just as in the natural, a son receives what the father has built, stewarded, and multiplied—so too in the spirit.

Proverbs 13:22 (NKJV) says, "A good man leaves an inheritance to his children's children."

This is not limited to financial legacy—it speaks of spiritual legacy. When you are covered by someone who has labored, travailed, and cultivated a well in the Spirit, you gain access to more than you could build alone.

Inheritance is not just about assets—it's about access.

There are wells of revival, revelation, healing, wisdom, prophetic insight, and authority that have been dug by spiritual mothers and fathers over decades. When you walk under their covering, you drink from those wells.

You don't have to start from scratch. You don't have to learn everything through failure. You can build on what has already been laid. This is the power of generational covering.

We often hear the phrase, "Each generation has to pay its own price." While there's truth in personal surrender, it's not biblical to reject spiritual inheritance. God is a generational God—Abraham, Isaac, and Jacob. And He delights in seeing sons go further than their fathers.

When you reject covering, you reject inheritance. When you embrace covering, you accelerate your journey. Coverings open doors. They release favor. They position you in ways you could not engineer on your own.

Conclusion: Receive the Covering—Walk in the Grace

Spiritual covering is not optional for the serious believer. It is essential. It is not just a safety net—it is a supply line. Without it, you can survive for a while. But eventually, the wear and tear of life, warfare, and confusion will leave you drained, isolated, and directionless.

But when you are covered...

- You are protected from the fiery darts of the enemy.
- You are affirmed in your identity and purpose.
- You are shaped through loving correction and sustained through prophetic encouragement.
- You are empowered through impartation.
- And you are positioned for inheritance.

This is the blessing of covering.

You were never meant to walk alone. You were never meant to carry the burden of your calling in isolation. God, in His wisdom and love, placed coverings in your life—not to suppress you, but to strengthen you. Not to control you, but to commission you.

So receive the covering. Honor the grace. Submit to the process. And watch as the fruit multiplies, the warfare lifts, and the anointing flows. The covering you honor determines the strength you walk in. The alignment you choose determines the inheritance you receive.

Discussion Questions

1 . Spiritual covering is described as both protective and empowering. In your own life, can you identify a time when you experienced either divine protection or spiritual encouragement through a relationship with a mentor, leader, or spiritual parent? How did that experience impact your faith journey?

2 . This chapter emphasizes that covering helps define identity and purpose through affirmation and accountability. Who in your life speaks identity over you? Are you currently in a position where someone helps refine your God-given purpose? If not, what steps can you take to pursue that kind of relationship?

3 . Correction is often uncomfortable but deeply necessary. How do you typically respond to correction—defensively or with a teachable heart? What would it look like to embrace correction as a form of love and protection rather than criticism or control?

5

CHARACTERISTICS OF A TRUE COVERING

In an age where leadership is often confused with dominance, and authority is distorted by manipulation, it is crucial that we recover the true characteristics of spiritual covering. Not every leader is a covering. Not every title-holder carries the heart of the Father. And not every influential voice in the church world has been entrusted with the spiritual responsibility of guarding, guiding, and growing others.

A true covering doesn't just look like authority—it feels like safety. It doesn't merely command submission—it invites trust. It doesn't position itself to be served—it lives to serve and protect. That is the nature of Christ, our ultimate covering, and that same character must be evident in anyone entrusted with spiritual authority over others.

This chapter explores four vital characteristics that must define a true covering:

- Love without control
- Strength without abuse

- Guidance without manipulation
- Sacrifice and intercession

Each of these qualities reveals the heart posture of someone who has been entrusted with the weight of another's spiritual journey. A true covering reflects Heaven's nature—not perfectly, but with humility and integrity.

1. Love Without Control

The foundation of any true covering is love—not just any love, but agape love: unconditional, patient, covenantal love that is not self-seeking or performance-based. Love is the anchor that secures the entire covering relationship. Without it, everything else becomes legalism, domination, or spiritual manipulation.

Love says, I am with you when you rise and when you fall. I see who you are and who you're becoming. I'm not here to control you—I'm here to serve your destiny.

Unfortunately, many have encountered "coverings" who used love as a lure, only to switch to control once loyalty was established. This is a counterfeit love—it is fear in disguise. True love releases rather than restricts. It builds up rather than boxes in. It draws out identity rather than forcing compliance.

Jesus demonstrated this love in His relationship with the disciples. He never manipulated them into obedience. He loved them in their weakness, corrected them in their pride, and washed their feet as their Lord and Teacher. His love did not control—it transformed.

When someone truly loves those they cover, they don't

demand submission—they win trust. Their love brings align-ment, not by force, but by spiritual gravity. People willingly stay under a covering when they know it is rooted in genuine affec-tion and covenantal love. A true covering doesn't measure someone's worth by performance. They do not withdraw when a son or daughter disappoints them.

Their love is not transactional—it is transformational.

2. Strength Without Abuse

The second characteristic of a true covering is strength that doesn't wound. Coverings must carry strength—emotional, spiritual, and moral strength. They must be stable in identity, mature in wisdom, and confident in their authority. But that strength must never cross the line into abuse.

True strength is not loud—it is consistent. It does not lord over—it lifts up. It is not insecure—it is anchored in grace. Coverings must be strong enough to lead others through crisis, confront sin when necessary, and carry the burden of spiritual responsibility. But strength, without humility and gentleness, becomes oppressive.

Paul wrote in 1 Thessalonians 2:7 (ESV), "We were gentle among you, like a nursing mother taking care of her own children."

What a beautiful picture of strength under control. Paul carried great authority, but it was expressed through gentleness and care. His strength didn't crush—it covered. Abuse happens when a leader uses their position to dominate, silence, or shame. That is not covering—it's control. And control is never the language of the Kingdom.

When spiritual leaders abuse their strength, they may build big ministries, but they leave behind broken sons and daughters—confused, wounded, and distrustful of authority. This is why strength must be married to meekness.

True strength sets boundaries, speaks truth, and provides stability. It does not erupt in rage. It does not threaten. It does not isolate or intimidate. It stands, even when others run. It fights for those under its care and refuses to abandon them. A strong covering absorbs pressure so those they lead can grow. They absorb criticism, take responsibility, and model resilience. Their strength is not a hammer—it's a shield.

3. Guidance Without Manipulation

Coverings must guide—but they must never manipulate. The difference lies in intent. Guidance points the way. Manipulation pressures you into a way. A true spiritual covering is there to offer wisdom, instruction, perspective, and counsel. But they leave the final decisions in the hands of the one they cover. They guide through relationship, not coercion.

Jesus modeled this beautifully. In John 6, after a hard teaching caused many disciples to leave, He looked at the twelve and said, "Do you also want to go away?" He didn't guilt them. He didn't twist their arms. He invited them to choose. That's guidance, not manipulation.

A manipulative leader will:

- Threaten to cut you off if you disagree
- Shame you for having questions
- Use guilt or fear to demand loyalty
- Turn others against you when you seek to leave

But a true covering will:

- Speak truth in love
- Leave room for your journey
- Celebrate your growth even if it takes you beyond their reach
- Remain available, even if you step away

Guidance empowers. Manipulation disables. Guidance says, *Here's what I sense God is doing—let's pray into it together.* Manipulation says, *If you don't do what I say, you're disobedient or rebellious.*

Coverings are stewards, not owners. They don't possess people—they prepare them for maturity and release. When you find a covering that offers guidance without control, hold them in high honor. They are rare—and they are the kind of leaders God is raising up to bring healing to a wounded generation.

4. Sacrifice and Intercession

Finally, a true covering is marked by sacrificial intercession. Covering is not merely administrative—it is priestly. A true covering doesn't just manage your journey—they carry you in prayer. They don't just advise you—they advocate for you in the spirit.

Moses stood between God's judgment and the people's sin and pleaded for mercy. Samuel cried out for Israel all night. Paul travailed in prayer "until Christ was formed" in his spiritual sons (Galatians 4:19). These were not casual leaders—they were coverings who carried others on their shoulders and in their hearts.

To cover someone is to take responsibility for them before God. It is to watch, to war, to weep, and to intercede. It is to feel their burdens as your own. It is to fast for their breakthrough, to pray for their clarity, and to contend for their future—even when they don't know you're doing it.

Sacrifice means availability. It means presence. It means carrying burdens in secret that others don't see. A true covering may not always have the perfect words, but they are always present in the Spirit.

Jesus did not just teach His disciples—He prayed for them. He interceded in John 17, asking the Father to keep them from the evil one, to sanctify them, to unify them, and to fill them with His glory. That's what coverings do—they pray what the Father wants over the lives of their sons and daughters.

Covering is not about perks—it's about pouring out. A true covering lays down their life so others can fulfill theirs.

What Happens When These Characteristics Are Missing?

When a spiritual leader lacks love, they become harsh and transactional. When they lack strength, they become passive and enable dysfunction. When they lack guidance, they become aimless or indulgent. And when they lack sacrifice, they become self-serving and detached.

The result? Sons and daughters are:

- Wounded rather than healed
- Confused rather than aligned
- Drifting rather than grounded

- Isolated rather than covered

This is why God is raising up true coverings in this hour. Not just gifted speakers or visionary leaders—but fathers and mothers who walk in these core characteristics. The Church does not need more titles. It needs more towels. It needs coverings who reflect the heart of the Great Shepherd and the Father of Lights.

How to Test and Discern a True Covering

You can recognize a true covering by the fruit they produce and the atmosphere they create. Ask yourself:

- Do I feel safe in their presence?
- Do they lead with love or with fear?
- Are they willing to correct me with grace and not shame?
- Do they pray for me, not just preach to me?
- Are they available, present, and invested in my growth?
- Do they celebrate my calling—even if it takes me beyond them?

A true covering builds sons and daughters, not just followers. They don't compete with your gift—they call it out. They don't build a monument to themselves—they raise up others to carry more than they did. And above all, they reflect the nature of Christ.

Conclusion: Coverings That Reflect the Father

The safest place to grow, develop, and be launched into your purpose is under the covering of someone who walks in love without control, strength without abuse, guidance without manipulation, and sacrifice with intercession. That kind of covering doesn't bind you—it blesses you. It doesn't limit you—it launches you.

You were never meant to walk alone, and you were never meant to be led by leaders who don't carry the Father's heart. God desires to connect every believer to coverings who reflect His character and reveal His nature. And as you mature, God may even call you to be that kind of covering for others.

So honor the coverings God has placed in your life. Discern their fruit. Stay aligned. And walk boldly in the protection, wisdom, and grace that true spiritual coverings provide. Because in the end, the covering over your life determines the climate you grow in—and the foundation you build from.

Discussion Questions

1 . Which of the four characteristics of a true spiritual covering—love without control, strength without abuse, guidance without manipulation, and sacrificial intercession—stood out to you the most, and why?

2 . How can you discern the difference between healthy spiritual guidance and manipulation in a leadership relationship?

3 . In what ways might God be calling you to become a covering for someone else?

6

THE FLOW OF THE ANOINTING THROUGH COVERING

One of the most misunderstood yet powerful realities of spiritual life is the flow of the anointing. The anointing is not simply a personal empowerment or emotional feeling. It is the tangible presence and power of God resting on a person to fulfill an assignment. But the anointing does not flow randomly. It flows through alignment, through submission, and through covering.

The same way oil flows through connected pipes in a system, the anointing flows through spiritual order. God's anointing rests upon headship, and it flows down through structures that are rightly aligned. This is why covering is not only about protection—it's about connection to power. Without proper alignment, the flow becomes hindered. With alignment, the oil flows freely.

In this chapter, we will explore:

- The biblical pattern of anointing flowing through covering

- Key examples: Elijah and Elisha, Moses and Joshua, Paul and Timothy
- How the anointing flows from head to body
- The importance of staying under the flow

The Principle of Flow

Psalm 133 gives us one of the clearest pictures of how the anointing flows:

"Behold, how good and pleasant it is for brethren to dwell together in unity! It is like the precious oil upon the head, running down on the beard, the beard of Aaron, running down on the edge of his garments... For there the Lord commanded the blessing—life forevermore." [Psalm 133:1-3 NKJV]

Here, unity is connected to anointing. And the anointing is connected to order and covering. The oil is poured on the head —Aaron, the high priest—and it flows down his beard and to the edge of his garments. This is a clear spiritual picture: God pours oil on the head, and as long as the body is connected to the head, it receives the flow.

If a part of the garment is disconnected, it does not receive the oil. This is the principle of divine flow: anointing flows through covering and alignment. It starts at the head—whether it be Christ as the Head of the Church, or a spiritual leader entrusted with oversight—and it continues downward, blessing everything that remains connected.

The moment a person disconnects from the covering God has placed in their life, the flow of the anointing is interrupted. They may still carry a measure of gift, charisma, or knowledge —but the divine weight of the anointing begins to wane.

Elijah and Elisha: Anointing Through Servanthood

The story of Elijah and Elisha is a textbook example of how anointing flows through covering. Elisha was a man plowing in a field when Elijah threw his mantle on him—a symbolic act of calling and invitation to alignment.

From that day forward, Elisha followed Elijah. He left his old life and became his servant. For years, he served Elijah—not just as a prophet-in-training, but as a son under covering. He poured water on Elijah's hands. He walked with him through cities. He stayed near when others stood at a distance.

Even when Elijah tried to dismiss him—"Stay here; the Lord has sent me to Bethel"—Elisha responded, "As surely as the Lord lives and you live, I will not leave you" (2 Kings 2:2 NIV).

That is the spirit of a son under covering. He refuses to break alignment. Why is this important?

Because when the time came for Elijah to be taken up into heaven, Elisha was in position. He had honored the process. He had remained under covering. And because of that, he received the double portion of Elijah's spirit.

Elijah said it clearly: "If you see me when I am taken from you, it will be yours." In other words: If you stay aligned, you'll receive the flow.

Elisha didn't get the double portion because he demanded it. He got it because he walked in honor, alignment, and submission. This is how anointing flows. Not through ambition, but through proximity, posture, and process.

Moses and Joshua: Anointing Through Laying on of Hands

Another example is Moses and Joshua. Joshua was Moses' assistant for decades. He lingered in the tent of meeting. He watched Moses navigate conflict, speak with God, and lead a stubborn people. And when the time came for leadership to transition, Moses didn't appoint Joshua because of a vote. He laid hands on him and imparted the anointing and wisdom that had rested on his own life.

Deuteronomy 34:9 (ESV) says: "Now Joshua the son of Nun was full of the spirit of wisdom, for Moses had laid his hands on him."

The transfer of wisdom and anointing came not through ambition, but through alignment and impartation. Joshua had walked with Moses, served Moses, and stayed connected. And when the time was right, the anointing flowed. Again, the pattern is clear: Stay aligned, stay connected, and you'll be positioned to receive the flow.

Paul and Timothy: Anointing Through Discipleship and Fatherhood

The New Testament gives us the example of Paul and Timothy. Paul was not just Timothy's teacher—he was a spiritual father. He called him "my true son in the faith" and "my beloved child." Paul didn't just give Timothy theology—he gave him his heart, his example, his prayers, and his authority.

In 2 Timothy 1:6 (NIV), Paul says: "Fan into flame the gift of God, which is in you through the laying on of my hands."

Here again we see a clear transfer—anointing flowing through alignment and covering. Timothy didn't just wake up with a ministry. He received something through connection. The gift was in him, but the stirring, maturing, and commissioning came through Paul's hands and voice.

Paul taught Timothy. He warned him. He commissioned him. And he reminded him that the grace and gift he carried didn't come from striving—it came through spiritual relationship and impartation.

The Head-to-Body Flow of Anointing

Returning to Psalm 133, let's revisit the powerful image of the anointing flowing from the head to the beard to the hem. This passage is a picture of the body of Christ. Christ is the Head. The anointing is poured on Him. And as we stay connected to the Head—and connected to those God has placed in delegated leadership—the anointing continues to flow.

But when parts of the body try to function independently of the Head—or when body parts separate from one another—the flow stops. This is why many believers live with frustration: they have calling but no clarity, gifting but no grace, hunger but no oil. They are attempting to walk in power while disconnected from covering.

The oil flows where there is order. The Spirit rests where there is unity. The power comes where there is submission. That's not religious control—it's Kingdom design.

You can be talented and still lack anointing.
You can be prophetic and still miss the weight of glory.
You can be platformed and still have no oil.

Because the oil is not guaranteed by visibility. It's sustained through submission, proximity, and humility.

Staying Under the Flow

The key to sustaining the anointing in your life is to stay under the flow. That means:

- Stay connected to Christ through intimacy
- Stay submitted to godly leadership
- Stay aligned with spiritual authority
- Stay faithful in hidden seasons
- Stay positioned in humility

When the oil flows, it brings clarity, healing, favor, and power. But you can't manipulate it. You can only receive it through alignment.

Some people start under covering, but eventually pride leads them to disconnect. They begin to believe they've outgrown their need for fathers, mentors, or spiritual oversight. They may continue for a while in the momentum of their past season—but eventually, the oil dries up.

Others disconnect because of offense. A correction comes. A disagreement arises. Instead of seeking reconciliation, they detach. But detachment always leads to drought.

If you want to walk in sustained anointing, you must be willing to walk in sustained alignment. That doesn't mean you'll never transition. But it does mean you'll never forsake covering out of pride or pain.

Signs That the Flow Is Hindered

How can you know if the anointing in your life has been hindered due to a break in covering? Here are some signs:

- Spiritual dryness despite consistent activity
- Confusion about next steps and calling
- Decreased authority in prayer or preaching
- Isolation from godly counsel
- Stagnation in growth, fruitfulness, or opportunities

The issue may not be gifting. It may be alignment. Sometimes a simple return to covering—reconnecting with those who've been assigned to you, repenting where needed, restoring honor—can restore the flow of grace and power in your life.

Conclusion: Stay in the Flow, Walk in the Power

The anointing is not earned—it is received. But it is only received when you are in position.

Elisha received the mantle because he stayed.
Joshua received the wisdom because he served.
Timothy walked in fire because he was fathered.

And you will receive the grace, power, and favor you need when you stay connected to the people God has assigned to your life as spiritual coverings.

The anointing flows from the head, through the body, to the hem. Don't disconnect and dry up. Don't isolate and miss the inheritance. Don't dishonor and disqualify yourself from the double portion.

Stay submitted.

Stay close.
Stay teachable.
Stay under the flow.

Because what you are connected to determines what flows into you—and what flows through you determines what God can entrust you with.

Discussion Questions

1. . Elisha, Joshua, and Timothy all received a spiritual inheritance by staying aligned under their leaders. What do their examples teach us about the difference between ambition and alignment? In what ways do you think God prepares us through the posture of servanthood before entrusting us with greater authority?

2. . Psalm 133 paints a picture of oil flowing from the head to the hem. Have you ever experienced spiritual dryness or stagnation that could be traced back to a disconnect in covering, unity, or alignment? How did you (or how can you) take steps to reconnect and get back under the flow?

3. . The chapter highlights that gifting, visibility, or passion do not guarantee anointing—only alignment does. Why do you think submission and spiritual authority are often resisted in today's culture, even within the church? What would it look like to cultivate a heart that values covering, correction, and humility?

7

HOW TO DISCERN THE RIGHT COVERING

N ot every leader is called to cover you. Not every pastor, apostle, prophet, or spiritual mentor is assigned to your journey. In the Kingdom, alignment is not about convenience—it's about divine appointment. Just as God assigns people for you to walk with in covenant, He also appoints coverings who are specifically graced to nurture, correct, equip, and protect you as you grow into maturity.

Finding the right covering is not just a matter of preference or style. It is a matter of discernment and destiny. To be covered rightly is to walk under a divine flow. To be covered wrongly—or uncovered altogether—is to walk vulnerable to deception, disconnection, and delay.

In this chapter, we'll explore three critical areas:

- Spiritual discernment and witness: Hearing God's voice in the selection of your covering
- Fruit over charisma: What to look for beyond giftings and popularity

- The safety of submission: Why the right covering brings security, not fear

This is not about fearfully judging others, but about being spiritually discerning so that you are aligned under the voice, grace, and mantle that is meant to speak into your life.

The Danger of Misalignment

Before we talk about discerning the right covering, let's be honest about the danger of submitting to the wrong one—or to no one at all.

Many believers are walking through spiritual burnout, prolonged warfare, chronic confusion, or cycles of sin not because they lack hunger or sincerity, but because they are either uncovered or misaligned. Either they've never had spiritual leadership speaking into their identity and direction, or they've submitted to leaders who operate in control, pride, or mixture. Both are dangerous.

To be uncovered is to be spiritually exposed. To be under a covering that is not clean is to absorb spiritual pollution. Just like sitting under a leaky or contaminated roof exposes you to toxins or storms, being under the wrong spiritual headship can:

- Invite confusion
- Nurture rebellion
- Distort doctrine
- Disrupt your divine timing
- Cause unnecessary wounds

This is why the right covering is critical for your development. It's not just about finding a church you enjoy—it's about finding a leader you're called to, someone whose grace flows into your life, and whose alignment brings protection and activation.

Spiritual Discernment and Witness

Discerning your covering begins in the spirit, not in the soul. Your soul may be drawn to a personality—someone who's funny, eloquent, or motivational. Your flesh may be attracted to comfort—leaders who never correct, challenge, or confront. But the Spirit of God within you knows who you are assigned to and who is assigned to you.

When David came to Samuel's house, the prophet nearly anointed the wrong brother—Eliab. He looked the part. He seemed strong. But God whispered,

"Do not look at his appearance or stature... for man looks at the outward appearance, but the Lord looks at the heart" (1 Samuel 16:7 NKJV).

That same truth applies to spiritual coverings. You must learn to discern not by appearance, gifting, or even external success—but by the witness of the Spirit.

Romans 8:16 says (NKJV), "The Spirit Himself bears witness with our spirit..."

That witness is often subtle. It's a deep knowing, a spiritual resonance that says, "This is someone God is using to shape me." You'll feel it when they speak—your spirit will leap. You'll sense divine order when they correct you—you won't rebel, you'll breathe easier. You'll notice a grace resting on them that covers your weakness and calls forth your destiny.

When you sense this witness:

- Take time in prayer and fasting to confirm it
- Observe the fruit over time, not just the moment
- Watch for peace that goes beyond logic
- Ask the Lord, "Is this the voice You've appointed to speak into my becoming?"

The right covering is not just about where you are—it's about where you're going. God assigns leaders who can see your future and prepare you for it.

Fruit Over Charisma

In Matthew 7:15–20 (ESV), Jesus gave a sobering warning: *"Beware of false prophets... You will recognize them by their fruits."*

He didn't say, "You'll know them by their gifts, following, or eloquence." He said: look at the fruit. Many believers fall into the trap of submitting to charisma rather than character. They align with voices that inspire the crowd but ignore the condition of the tree producing that fruit.

Ask these questions before aligning under someone's spiritual covering:

- Do they walk in humility or pride?
- Are they under covering themselves?
- Do they produce healthy disciples or just fans?
- Is their doctrine sound and rooted in Scripture?
- Do they demonstrate the fruit of the Spirit (love, patience, self-control)?
- Is there a consistent track record of integrity?

You may enjoy someone's preaching, but that doesn't mean they are assigned to cover your soul. A true covering is not simply a conference speaker or online influencer—they are someone you can walk with, be accountable to, and be fathered by. Their fruit will bear that out over time.

Sometimes the most anointed coverings don't have the largest platforms. They carry oil, wisdom, and a track record in the Spirit—but they may be hidden in local churches, walking humbly with a few rather than parading before the many.

Discern the fruit. Don't rush. Don't force alignment out of hype or emotion. Let time and fruit confirm the witness you sense in your spirit.

The Safety of Submission

Submission has become a scary word for many, especially those who have experienced spiritual abuse, authoritarian leadership, or manipulative control. But submission, when done rightly and to the right people, is not only safe—it is liberating.

Submission does not mean blind obedience or loss of identity. It means choosing to come under the grace and authority of someone God has appointed to help shape and protect your destiny.

In Hebrews 13:17 (ESV), we read, "Obey your leaders and submit to them, for they are keeping watch over your souls, as those who will give an account..."

This Scripture reveals the weight of the covering relationship. True leaders watch over souls—not just sermons. They carry a heavenly accountability for your development. Submission, then, is not about control—it's about covering. And when you are rightly submitted:

- You walk in peace
- You receive protection in warfare
- You're less vulnerable to deception
- You receive correction in love, not condemnation
- You grow in character, not just calling

Submission should never feel like bondage. It should feel like security. It's the sense that you are not walking alone. You're not spiritually homeless. You're not fending for yourself. Someone is praying for you, watching over your soul, and helping you walk the narrow road.

If your submission to someone produces fear, manipulation, or constant anxiety, you are likely not under the right covering. But if your submission leads to peace, clarity, humility, and growth—even when you're corrected—you've likely found a divine assignment.

What the Right Covering Looks Like

Let's summarize some of the marks of a right covering. These traits, which you'll find echoed in the earlier chapters of this book, will help you practically identify who God may be assigning to your life.

1. **They see who you are becoming, not just where you've been.** A true covering doesn't reduce you to your past. They speak to your potential. They help you mature into your calling. They don't compete with you—they prepare you.

2. **They carry grace for your weakness.** You feel strengthened in their presence. Even when corrected, you don't feel condemned—you feel redirected. They carry a burden for your soul.

3. **They are accountable themselves.** They are not rogue. They are not isolated. They live under covering and community. They model the submission they call others to.

4. **They teach sound doctrine and walk in humility.** They aren't moved by trends. Their foundation is the Word. Their lifestyle reflects holiness and servanthood.

5. **They make time for sons, not just fans.** They are not just building crowds—they're building people. They have capacity for relationship, not just platform ministry.

What to Do If You're Uncovered

If you're reading this and realizing that you are not currently under a spiritual covering, don't be discouraged—be intentional.

Here are some practical steps to take:

1. Pray earnestly.
Ask the Holy Spirit to reveal who He has assigned to walk with you. Don't just look around—look up. He will guide you.

2. Seek with humility.
Avoid prideful independence. Be willing to receive correction and to trust God's timing.

3. Observe before you submit.
Don't rush into covenant. Take time to observe fruit, ask questions, and watch how they lead others.

4. Initiate the conversation.
If you sense someone is a possible covering, don't wait for them to approach you. Reach out. Express your heart and desire for accountability and relationship.

5. Commit, don't consume.
The right covering isn't a service provider—it's a relationship. Show up. Serve. Honor. Submit. Lean in. Let your life be seen.

Conclusion: Covered by Divine Assignment
Who covers you is not just a theological question—it's a spiritual alignment decision that will impact your destiny. God never intended for you to be spiritually homeless, self-governed, or without oversight.

He loves you enough to appoint voices to speak into your identity, grace to carry you in warfare, and fathers to guide you in maturity. But it's your responsibility to discern that covering—to listen to the Spirit, test the fruit, and embrace the process of submission.

When you come under the right covering:

- Your growth accelerates
- Your identity is affirmed
- Your purpose is clarified
- Your battles are no longer yours alone
- And your inheritance becomes accessible

The right covering is a gift. It is not always loud or glamorous, but it is anointed, safe, and essential. So pray. Discern. Submit. And walk confidently—because when you're under the right covering, you're in the right flow.

Discussion Questions

1. What does it mean to be "spiritually aligned" with the right covering, and how can misalignment affect your growth?

2. How can you discern the difference between charisma and true spiritual fruit when choosing a covering?

3. In what ways should godly submission feel safe and freeing, rather than controlling or fearful?

8

SONS WHO WANT COVERING

There is a deep ache in the Body of Christ today—not just for purpose, power, or position, but for belonging. Hidden beneath many questions believers ask about leadership, mentorship, and spiritual oversight is a heart-cry that says, "Will someone walk with me? Will someone see me, cover me, father me?"

Not every believer has the vocabulary for this longing, but the Spirit knows the language. What they are longing for is covering. And more specifically, they are longing to be sons—not orphans trying to prove themselves, but sons and daughters secure in identity, open to correction, and eager to be aligned under fatherly guidance.

But not all sons want covering—at least, not at first. For many, the journey toward healthy spiritual covering is first a journey of inner healing, where the orphan spirit must be broken and the heart made ready to trust again.

This chapter explores:

- The orphan spirit vs. the spirit of sonship
- The resistance to covering (rebellion, independence, and mistrust)
- The healing required to truly receive covering

The Orphan Spirit vs. The Spirit of Sonship

Every person is born into a spiritual war. From the beginning, the enemy has sought to fracture family and distort identity. He knows that if he can sever the connection between sons and fathers—both naturally and spiritually—he can keep people in a state of striving, insecurity, and spiritual homelessness. The result is what many have called the orphan spirit.

An orphan spirit is not about natural parenthood; it is a spiritual condition. It is the mindset that believes:

- I'm on my own.
- No one sees me.
- I have to protect myself.
- I can't trust leaders.
- I must prove my value through performance.

In contrast, the spirit of sonship says:

- I belong.
- I am seen, known, and loved.
- I am protected by God and spiritual family.
- I am not alone—I walk under covering.
- I don't have to prove my worth; it has been declared by my Father.

Romans 8:15 says, "You did not receive the spirit of slavery to fall back into fear, but you have received the Spirit of adoption as sons."

This adoption is not theoretical. It's deeply practical. It means you no longer have to live as a spiritual orphan—you can live as a secure son who trusts the Father and honors His order.

Yet many believers carry orphan mindsets while crying out for sonship. They long for a father figure but reject correction. They desire mentorship but resent authority. They crave belonging but isolate when challenged. The tension is real—and it must be confronted if we are to truly receive the gift of covering.

Rebellion, Independence, and Mistrust: The Enemies of Sonship

To embrace covering, we must confront the internal barriers that keep us spiritually homeless. Three of the greatest barriers are rebellion, independence, and mistrust. These are not just emotional reactions; they are spiritual postures that must be surrendered.

1. Rebellion: The Root of Resistance

Rebellion is not just outward disobedience—it is inward resistance to authority. It often masks itself in spiritual language: "I just follow God, not man." "I don't want to be controlled." "God can speak to me directly." While there's truth to each of those statements, rebellion twists them into justifications for avoidance.

The root of rebellion is usually pain. Somewhere along the line, leadership disappointed, manipulated, or wounded the person. Instead of healing, the heart hardened. Instead of trusting again, walls were built. But rebellion, no matter how justified it feels, always produces distance, not covering.

Rebellion resists correction. It interprets challenge as control. It demands its own way but secretly longs for direction. The only cure for rebellion is repentance and trust in God's order. God doesn't demand submission because He's insecure —He calls us to submit because order brings safety, and honor unlocks inheritance.

2. Independence: The Illusion of Strength

Independence is often celebrated in Western culture. But spiritual independence is a dangerous illusion. No one in Scripture fulfilled their assignment alone—not even Jesus. He walked in submission to the Father and chose to walk in community.

Independence says:

- "I don't need anyone."
- "I'll figure it out on my own."
- "I've been burned before—so I'll do it myself."

But isolation doesn't produce maturity. It leads to deception, stagnation, and burnout. Many people who claim independence are not actually free—they're just wounded and unhealed.

True strength is not found in isolation—it's found in alignment. Sons who walk in humility and connection go farther, last longer, and stand stronger.

3. Mistrust: The Wound That Keeps You Guarded

Mistrust is the natural consequence of betrayal. When spiritual leaders abuse power, abandon responsibility, or walk in hypocrisy, those under them feel unsafe—and rightly so. But mistrust that goes unhealed becomes a lens through which all future relationships are filtered.

Mistrust whispers:

- "They'll all eventually hurt you."
- "If you let them in, they'll control you."
- "You're better off alone."

But mistrust, if left unchecked, becomes a self-fulfilling prophecy. It leads to guarded relationships, unteachable attitudes, and shallow community. Healing doesn't mean pretending the pain didn't happen. It means acknowledging it, grieving it, and inviting God to rewire your ability to trust again.

Covering requires vulnerability. You cannot be covered if you remain hidden behind emotional armor.

Healing to Receive Covering

Healing is not a prerequisite for being covered—but it is a requirement for truly receiving from your covering. Many people come under spiritual leadership but never open their heart. They remain guarded, skeptical, or rebellious—and as a result, they miss the grace that covering is meant to release.

So how do you heal?

1. Acknowledge the Wound
Don't spiritualize it. Don't bury it. Name it. Who hurt you? What happened? What beliefs did it produce in

you? Healing begins with honesty. God cannot heal what we won't admit.

2. Forgive the Offender

Forgiveness is not excusing. It's releasing. You let go of the right to punish so that you can walk in freedom. Forgiveness doesn't always restore relationship—but it always restores you.

3. Grieve What Was Lost

Grieve the years without covering. Grieve the betrayal. Grieve the absence of fatherly protection. God meets you in your mourning. He's not rushing you—He's sitting with you.

4. Invite God to Rebuild Trust

Ask Him to heal your heart and guide you to the right covering. Let Him show you what spiritual family is supposed to look like. He is the restorer of the breach.

5. Take Steps Toward Vulnerability

You don't have to trust blindly. But you do need to start taking steps. Open up. Share your story. Ask questions. Allow someone into your journey again.

Healing doesn't happen in isolation—it happens in safe spiritual family, under the grace of spiritual fathers and mothers.

What Sons Who Want Covering Look Like

When healing begins, and the spirit of sonship starts to replace the orphan spirit, certain fruits begin to emerge. Sons who want covering are not perfect, but they carry a different posture. Here are some marks:

- They ask for feedback and correction. They don't run from accountability—they pursue it.
- They serve joyfully. They aren't looking to build their own platform. They're eager to be part of a vision bigger than themselves.
- They express gratitude and honor. They're quick to celebrate their leaders and coverers.
- They walk in humility. They're not constantly asserting themselves. They're content to grow in hiddenness if that's what the season requires.
- They initiate relationship. They don't wait to be chased down—they seek connection and alignment.

Most importantly, they don't expect perfection from their covering—they just look for purity, presence, and protection.

God Loves the Cry for Covering

Heaven responds to the cry of a heart that says, "God, connect me with those who will cover me." When you begin to walk in sonship, you're not just looking for a title—you're looking for covenant. And God delights to answer that prayer.

Psalm 68:6 says, "God sets the solitary in families..." If you've felt spiritually alone, wandering from one place to another, confused about who you're assigned to, God wants to bring you home—not just to a church, but to a covering.

The question is not, "Is there a father for me?" The question is, "Am I becoming a son who's ready to be covered?"

Conclusion: The Rise of Sons

The earth is not crying out for more preachers, programs, or personalities. Romans 8:19 says, "The creation waits in eager expectation for the sons of God to be revealed."

Sons—not orphans.
Sons who are healed.
Sons who are humble.
Sons who are covered.
Sons who know who they are and whose they are.

You are called to be one of those sons or daughters. You don't have to stay hidden. You don't have to stay guarded. You don't have to walk alone.

There is a covering for you.

But more importantly, there is a spirit of sonship waiting to be awakened inside of you. Receive healing. Reject rebellion. Renounce independence. Forgive the past. And begin walking as a son who wants to be covered.

Because covered sons become powerful leaders. Covered sons become fathers. Covered sons build safe places for the next generation.

Discussion Questions

1. What does the difference between an orphan spirit and the spirit of sonship reveal about how we see ourselves and God?

2. What barrier—rebellion, independence, or mistrust—has been the hardest for you to surrender, and why?

3. How can you begin walking as a son or daughter who is ready to be covered?

9

BECOMING A COVERING FOR OTHERS

You weren't just born to be covered—you were born to become a covering. The journey of sonship leads to the call of fatherhood. Everyone begins as a son or daughter, learning to walk in alignment, humility, and submission. But as you grow in maturity and faithfulness, the Lord begins to entrust you with others—sons and daughters, disciples and leaders, those who need your wisdom, prayer, and spiritual protection.

Spiritual fathering isn't about age. It's not just for those with gray hair and decades of experience. It's about maturity, humility, and a burden to cover others in love and truth. In a fatherless generation—both naturally and spiritually—God is calling many into the sacred role of covering others. This is not a role of control or domination. It is a responsibility born from love and a heart that carries others in prayer, correction, and covenant.

In this chapter, we'll explore:

- When God calls you to father
- Covering as responsibility, not control
- Raising others while remaining under covering yourself

The Call to Father

There comes a moment in every maturing believer's life when God shifts the question from "Who's covering me?" to "Who am I called to cover?" You realize that your growth was never just about your own breakthrough—it was preparation to become a spiritual shelter for others.

Paul writes to the Corinthians, "Though you have countless guides in Christ, you do not have many fathers. For I became your father in Christ Jesus through the gospel" (1 Corinthians 4:15). This is more than mentorship or leadership—it is spiritual fatherhood. A father takes personal responsibility for the growth, development, and destiny of another.

The call to father doesn't always come with a dramatic moment or audible word. Often, it begins with a burden. You notice someone struggling. You feel responsible for their growth. You begin to pray for them. You find yourself pouring out wisdom, inviting them in, correcting in love, and covering them in prayer.

That's the seed of fatherhood. And if it's from the Lord, it will grow. God may call you to father one or many. Some are called to cover a spiritual son or daughter in their home, a small group of leaders, or a generation of voices. But no matter the size, the weight is sacred. You are standing in the gap for someone else's future.

The call to father is not a call to control someone's life—it's a call to lay your life down so someone else can flourish.

The Difference Between Control and Covering

One of the most dangerous distortions of spiritual fatherhood is control masquerading as covering. A true father protects; a false father possesses. A true covering empowers; a false covering manipulates. As we respond to God's call to become coverings for others, we must be vigilant to walk in servanthood, not superiority.

Control says:

- "Do what I say, or you're out."
- "I know what's best for you in every situation."
- "You need me to hear God for you."

Covering says:

- "Let's walk together and seek God's wisdom."
- "I'll guide you, but I'll also empower you to choose."
- "I trust God's Spirit in you—and I'll stand with you in the process."

Control isolates. Covering includes.
Control demands. Covering disciples.
Control hoards influence. Covering releases sons.

Control creates spiritual orphans who fear leadership. Covering builds sons and daughters who know how to walk in freedom under authority. As a covering, you are not God. You are not the Holy Spirit. You are a voice, not the only voice. You are a guide, not a dictator. You are a protector, not a puppeteer.

Paul never demanded that Timothy obey him blindly. Instead, he taught, corrected, encouraged, and equipped. He said things like,

"What you have heard from me... entrust to faithful men" (2 Timothy 2:2 ESV)

That's a fathering spirit—multiplying wisdom, not controlling sons.

If God entrusts you with someone's heart, never abuse it. If He entrusts you with their process, never rush it. If He gives you influence, use it to build them—not your own image. The greatest test of your fathering is how free your sons feel to grow, ask, and even disagree—without fear of rejection.

What a Spiritual Covering Provides

As we step into the role of covering, it's essential to know what our sons and daughters need. They don't need another celebrity voice. They don't need more correction without compassion. They need presence, prayer, patience, and truth.

Here are some of the vital roles you fulfill as a spiritual covering:

1. Affirmation of Identity
Your voice as a father will often be the first voice someone hears confirming their identity. Just as the Father spoke over Jesus at baptism—"You are My beloved Son, in whom I am well pleased"—you are called to speak identity before performance, and affirmation before achievement.

2. Intercession in Warfare

You are not just a mentor. You are a priest. You stand in the gap for those under your covering. You fight for them in prayer. You bear their burdens. Their break-through becomes your battle. You don't just give advice —you contend.

3. Correction Without Rejection

There will be moments you must speak hard truths. But true fathers correct without cutting off. You rebuke in love. You restore after failure. You model repentance yourself. Your correction builds up, not beats down.

4. Release into Purpose

Sons and daughters are not meant to stay under you forever. They are meant to be launched. Your goal is not to keep them dependent—it's to send them strong, secure, and ready. You rejoice when they go farther than you.

The heart of a covering is not "How long can you serve me?" but "How well can I serve your destiny?"

Raising Others While Remaining Under Covering

A common trap for leaders who begin to cover others is the temptation to step out from under covering themselves. As you become a father, don't stop being a son. As you cover others, don't become isolated. As you build, don't stop being built into.

Jesus walked with authority, but never apart from the Father. He said, "I do nothing on My own. I only do what I see the Father doing" (John 5:19 ESV). That's the posture of a son who is a covering—leading with authority, but never disconnected from alignment.

You are never too mature to need covering. You may father many—but you still need someone praying for you, correcting you, and asking you the hard questions.

Remaining under covering while covering others protects you from:

- Burnout
- Pride
- Isolation
- Doctrinal drift
- Emotional exhaustion

It also models health to those you lead. Your sons and daughters will learn to value covering if they see you living under it yourself.

Be honest about your need for accountability. Be open to correction from your own covering. Stay aligned. Stay teachable. Don't just talk about covering—live it.

Signs You Are Called to Cover Others

If you're wondering whether God is calling you into this role, consider the following signs:

- You feel a growing burden for others' spiritual growth, not just your own.
- People naturally come to you for wisdom, prayer, or direction.

- You feel responsible for the atmosphere of purity, truth, and spiritual order in your house or ministry.
- You are more concerned about their future than your recognition.
- You pray for them privately, not just lead them publicly.
- You've matured through your own process of being fathered and now feel a call to reproduce.

You don't need a title to start covering. You need a heart that says, "I'll carry them like the Father carried me."

The Reward of Covering Others

Covering others isn't always easy. It involves sacrifice, long nights, disappointment, and deep commitment. But the reward is eternal.

- When your spiritual son preaches his first message, you'll weep like it was yours.
- When your daughter breaks free from addiction, your intercession will have been worth it.
- When those you raised become leaders themselves, you'll rejoice—not because they made you famous, but because they were launched into purpose.

Paul wrote to the Thessalonians, "For what is our hope, our joy, or the crown in which we will glory in the presence of our Lord Jesus when He comes? Is it not you?" (1 Thessalonians 2:19)

That is the reward of covering: People. Legacy. Sons and daughters walking in freedom and power.

Conclusion: A Generation of Coverings

If the Church is going to thrive in the days ahead, we need more than teachers—we need fathers and mothers. We need pastors, apostles, leaders, and everyday believers who say, "I'll carry the next generation."

God is raising up a generation of coverings—sons who became fathers, disciples who now disciple others, leaders who walk in humility and love.

You don't have to be perfect to cover someone. You just have to be present, prayerful, and submitted. You need to carry the heart of the Father, and the willingness to say, "You're not alone. I've got you. I'll walk with you into your destiny."

So rise up. Take the towel. Stand in the gap. And become the covering you once longed for—because there's a generation waiting for someone to cover them in the day of battle.

Discussion Questions

1. What does it mean to "shift from being covered to becoming a covering," and how can you recognize when that shift is happening in your own life?

2. How can you tell the difference between spiritual control and true covering in your leadership or the leadership you're under?

3. Why is it essential to remain under covering even as you begin to cover others? What does healthy mutual submission look like?

10

THE COST OF BEING UNCOVERED

Covering is not a luxury—it's a lifeline. In the realm of the Spirit, no one thrives in isolation. No one walks in lasting victory, growth, or protection without proper alignment under the authority God has ordained. When a believer or a leader rejects covering, whether through rebellion, pride, fear, or ignorance, the result is not freedom—it's exposure.

To be uncovered is to walk outside the protective order of God. It's to place yourself in spiritual danger. It may feel freeing for a moment—but it always costs more than you can afford.

In this chapter, we will explore:

- Stories of spiritual downfall caused by lack of covering
- What happens when people break rank
- How uncovering leads to exposure
- The warning signs of drifting out from under covering

- God's invitation to come back under spiritual protection

Uncovered: The First Sin in the Garden

The cost of being uncovered begins in Genesis. Adam and Eve were covered—physically, spiritually, and relationally. They walked in innocence, aligned under God's voice and authority. But the moment they sinned, they lost covering. Genesis 3:7 says, "Then the eyes of both of them were opened, and they realized they were naked."

Before this moment, they were physically naked but spiritually covered. After sin entered, the spiritual covering lifted—and shame rushed in. Their first instinct was to hide, to sew fig leaves together, and to avoid the presence of God. This is what happens when someone becomes uncovered:

- Shame replaces intimacy
- Hiding replaces honesty
- Fear replaces confidence
- Separation replaces alignment

The Garden is more than a history lesson—it's a spiritual pattern. To step out of God's covering is to step into exposure. The enemy has not changed his tactics. He tempts people out of covering with a lie: "You'll be more powerful if you're free to do things your own way." But he never tells them that uncovering leads to spiritual death.

Breaking Rank: The Story of Korah

In Numbers 16, we find a sobering account of a group of leaders who chose to step out from divine order. Korah, along with Dathan, Abiram, and 250 other leaders, confronted Moses and Aaron, saying, "You take too much upon yourselves... the whole congregation is holy."

At first glance, it sounds like a call for equality. But beneath their words was rebellion. They were not calling for humility in leadership—they were rejecting the authority God had established. What happened next is terrifying: the ground opened up and swallowed them alive.

Why? Because they broke rank. They stepped out from the covering God had appointed and walked into judgment. This is not just Old Testament severity—it's a timeless spiritual principle: those who reject covering place themselves in harm's way.

There's a reason armies have ranks. There's a reason sheep stay close to the shepherd. And there's a reason spiritual families are ordered with fathers, leaders, and coverings. To break rank is to break protection. You may still be gifted. You may still be anointed. But once you reject covering, you are on your own.

The Tragedy of King Uzziah

Uzziah was a young and powerful king. He reigned in Jerusalem for fifty-two years. He loved God, built cities, won battles, and sought the Lord early in his reign. But at the height of his success, something shifted.

2 Chronicles 26:16 (ESV) says, "But when he was strong, his heart was lifted up, to his destruction."

He entered the temple to burn incense on the altar—something only priests were allowed to do. Azariah the priest and eighty others tried to stop him, but Uzziah refused correction.

In that moment, he stepped out of covering. He broke spiritual protocol. He dishonored authority. Immediately, leprosy broke out on his forehead, and he lived the rest of his life in isolation.

This is the price of presumption. Uzziah wasn't judged for seeking God—he was judged for violating divine order. His gift made room for him, but his pride made him vulnerable. He believed he no longer needed covering. The result? Exposure, disease, and exile.

Let this be a warning to every leader, pastor, and rising voice in the Kingdom: your gift can take you where your covering was meant to sustain you. Don't let success seduce you out of submission.

Uncovering in the New Testament: The Sons of Sceva

In Acts 19, we read about the sons of Sceva—Jewish exorcists who tried to imitate the ministry of Paul. They said to a demon,

"In the name of Jesus whom Paul preaches, I command you to come out." But the demon replied, "Jesus I know, and Paul I know, but who are you?"(Acts 19: 13-15 NIV)

Then the man with the evil spirit attacked them, leaving them bleeding and naked.

Why did this happen?

Because the sons of Sceva tried to operate in authority without alignment. They had language but no covering. They used the right name, but had no right relationship. They invoked Jesus' name without walking under His lordship—and without submission to spiritual oversight.

The demon recognized authority—and they had none. In the spirit realm, unauthorized use of spiritual power is dangerous. Without covering, you are vulnerable to attack. Warfare is real, and only those under authority can walk in authority.

What Happens When You're Uncovered

Being uncovered may not lead to immediate crisis. In fact, it may feel exciting at first. There's no one telling you what to do. You're calling your own shots. You're living "free."But slowly, almost invisibly, the cost begins to show.

1. Deception Increases
Without covering, your discernment begins to dull. You are more likely to believe error, entertain strange doctrines, or become spiritually prideful. The voices around you no longer confront you—they flatter you. And truth becomes flexible.

2. Warfare Intensifies
You start getting hit harder—mentally, emotionally, relationally. Things that used to be easy now become hard. Your prayers feel dry. Your authority is thin. That's because you've lost your covering in the spirit. The enemy has access where protection once stood.

3. Fruitfulness Diminishes
What once was fruitful begins to feel forced. You may still be working, but the grace is gone. Ideas dry up. Connections break down. Doors close. You're still gifted

—but something is missing. That something is spiritual alignment.

4. Relationships Fracture

Uncovered people often attract other uncovered people. The result? Shallow connections, mistrust, and division. There's no shared accountability. Everyone's "doing their own thing," and spiritual sons and daughters begin to scatter.

5. Exposure Happens

Eventually, the hidden becomes visible. Sin that was once private becomes public. The cracks in your character get revealed. The flaws that a father or mother could have addressed in private now explode in public.

This is the final cost of being uncovered: exposure.

Proverbs 29:1 says, "He who is often reproved, yet stiffens his neck, will suddenly be broken beyond healing." (ESV)

God gives time. He sends warnings. He sends fathers. But when covering is repeatedly rejected, exposure becomes inevitable.

Warning Signs You're Drifting Out of Covering

- You no longer seek counsel or accountability
- You avoid correction
- You resent authority figures
- You feel isolated or spiritually dry
- You begin justifying disconnection
- You elevate personal "revelation" over biblical order
- You question the need for spiritual family

These are red flags. Don't ignore them. Don't call it "just a season." Call it what it is: a drift toward uncovering. And let the Holy Spirit bring you back before the storm hits.

The Mercy of God in Exposure

Even when exposure happens, it's not the end of the story. Exposure is not always God's judgment—it's often His mercy. When God exposes, He's not trying to destroy you. He's trying to bring you back. Better to be exposed and restored than to die in deception.

In Luke 15, the prodigal son walked away from the covering of his father's house. He squandered his inheritance, lost his dignity, and ended up feeding pigs. But when he came to himself, he said, "I will arise and go to my father."

The father ran to meet him, restored his robe, gave him a ring, and brought him back into the house. This is the heart of God: restoration, not rejection. If you've walked away from covering—whether out of pride, pain, or ignorance—there's a way back.

The Invitation to Return

God is calling His sons and daughters back under covering. He's calling leaders back to submission. He's calling gifted but isolated voices back into alignment. The cost of being uncovered is too high to ignore. But the gift of covering is still available.

If you've been uncovered:

- Repent. Not in shame, but in surrender.

- Forgive. Release those who failed you.
- Ask. Seek the Lord for the right covering and spiritual family.
- Submit. Humbly re-enter relationship and accountability.
- Heal. Let God restore what was broken.

You are not meant to walk alone. You are not meant to carry your calling unprotected. And you don't have to prove your worth outside of covering. God's way is still the best way.

Conclusion: Cover Me in the Day of Battle

There will always be a day of battle. A moment when your strength runs low. When the enemy comes in like a flood. When your discernment is cloudy. When your emotions are heavy. When your soul is weary. And in that moment, the question will be: *Who covers you?*

Don't wait for crisis to seek covering. Don't wait until you've fallen. Don't wait until you've burned out. Seek it now. Stay aligned now. Walk covered now. *Because the cost of being uncovered is never worth the price.*

Let the cry of your heart be, "Cover me in the day of battle." Because when you're covered, you're not just protected—you're positioned for victory.

Discussion Questions

1 . Why do you think spiritual covering is often resisted, and
what lies fuel that resistance?

2 . What are some warning signs that you—or someone you
know—might be drifting out from under spiritual
covering?

3 . How does God's mercy show up even in moments of
exposure, and why is restoration under covering more
powerful than operating in isolation?

11

WARFARE AND THE DAY OF BATTLE

E veryone faces battles—but not everyone is covered when the battle comes.

The day of battle is not hypothetical. It's real. It's spiritual. It's personal. Whether it's a wave of discouragement, a family crisis, a season of demonic attack, or a moment of decision that shapes destiny—everyone will face a day where the war intensifies. And when that day comes, the question will not be how strong you feel or how much Scripture you know. The question will be: Who is covering you?

In the day of battle, you don't need a crowd—you need a covering. You need someone who sees your blind spots, carries your burdens, discerns your season, and contends for your future. Covering is not just a matter of order. In the heat of war, it becomes a matter of life or death.

This chapter explores:

- Why covering matters most in crisis

- The prayers of a father in the battle
- Standing in the gap for sons and daughters

The Day of Battle Is Inevitable

There is a reason Scripture says,

"Put on the full armor of God, so that when the day of evil comes, you may be able to stand your ground" (Ephesians 6:13 NIV).

Not if, but when. Every believer will face an intense season of spiritual conflict.

The day of battle may look different for each of us:

- A sudden betrayal that shakes your trust
- A moral temptation that comes with unusual force
- A demonic assignment against your mind, marriage, or ministry
- A moment where you're forced to choose between obedience and compromise
- A season of silence where God feels distant and warfare is constant

In those moments, isolation is dangerous. You can't cover yourself in a war you were never meant to fight alone.

There are some battles that only fathers can fight. Some storms that only shepherds can rebuke. Some attacks that only fall under the weight of intercession and alignment.

Without covering, you may survive—but you will not prevail. The enemy doesn't fear your independence—he fears your alignment. He fears the person who knows how to run to their covering and say, "Pray for me. Speak over me. Stand with me."

When David Covered His Men in Battle

In 2 Samuel 18, David's army prepared for battle against his rebellious son Absalom. The people said to David,

> *"You must not go out to battle with us. If we lose, they'll come for you. Stay back and cover us from the city." (NIV)*

David, the warrior king, stayed behind—not out of fear, but to cover his men from behind the scenes.

There's a lesson here: covering doesn't always look like the front lines. Sometimes the greatest warfare happens in the hidden place, through the words, prayers, and discernment of the one who watches and weeps from the high tower.

True covering knows when to lead publicly and when to war privately. When a father stays back to pray, watch, and give instruction—it becomes a strategy for survival. His presence in the background is the reason others can advance on the field.

Don't underestimate the power of spiritual covering in the shadows. Often, your victory in the battle isn't because of what you did—it's because someone covered you while you fought.

The Prayers of a Father in the Battle

There's a kind of prayer that only comes from a father. Not a casual prayer. Not a religious repetition. But a travailing cry—a groan of the spirit that covers sons and daughters in the day of battle.

Paul said to the Galatians, "I am again in the pains of child-birth until Christ is formed in you" (Galatians 4:19). That's what a spiritual covering does—they carry you in intercession until Christ is formed and the battle is won.

There are times when your faith is low, and you can't see straight. But your covering prays. They see what you can't see. They discern the assignment, break the stronghold, and speak words that turn the tide.

Elijah prayed for rain while his servant looked for clouds. Again and again, Elijah bowed low until breakthrough came. That's the image of a covering in battle—head down, knees bent, mouth open, petitioning heaven on your behalf.

You may not hear them praying.
You may not feel the shift at first.
But make no mistake: things are moving in the spirit
because someone is covering you

This is why uncovering is so dangerous. Without someone praying for you in battle, the pressure builds, the attacks escalate, and your discernment begins to dull. Covered sons walk with reinforcements. Uncovered ones walk exposed.

Moses, Aaron, and Hur: A Covering That Sustains Victory

One of the clearest pictures of spiritual covering in warfare comes from Exodus 17. As Joshua fought the Amalekites in the valley, Moses stood on the hill with the staff of God in his hands. As long as Moses' hands were lifted, Israel prevailed. But when his arms grew tired and dropped, the enemy gained ground.

So Aaron and Hur came beside Moses and held up his hands—one on each side—until the sun went down. This is the power of spiritual covering in the day of battle:

- Someone is lifting their hands in intercession.
- Others are lifting their hands to sustain his.
- Victory comes not just from the sword in the valley —but from the hands lifted on the hill.

In spiritual battles, we need more than strategy—we need intercession and alignment. We need spiritual fathers and mothers holding up our arms. We need coverings who know when we're tired, who discern the warfare before we speak it, and who sustain us when we're weak.

The victory in the valley was a result of the posture on the hill.

The Strategy of the Enemy: Isolate and Attack

Satan is a strategist. He doesn't just oppose randomly—he attacks strategically. One of his favorite tactics? Isolation.

Lions don't attack the center of the herd. They go for the straggler. The one who drifts. The one who distances. The one who refuses to come under covering.

1 Peter 5:8 reminds us, "Your enemy the devil prowls around like a roaring lion looking for someone to devour." (NIV)

Not everyone—someone. Who? The isolated. The unaligned. The uncovered.

The enemy isn't afraid of your potential—he's afraid of your position. He knows that as long as you stay covered, you are guarded, protected, and reinforced. But if he can get you uncovered—through offense, pride, fear, or shame—he can wear you out and wipe you out.

This is why people fall in the middle of ministry.
This is why leaders collapse under pressure.
This is why sons and daughters wander and wither.

They lost their covering.

The Covering in Gethsemane

When Jesus approached the cross, He didn't isolate—He invited His inner circle to pray with Him. "Stay here and keep watch with Me." Even Jesus desired covering in the day of battle.

He wasn't asking for protection—He was modeling intercession in proximity. Jesus wanted someone near Him in the agony of Gethsemane. And when His disciples fell asleep, He returned to them and said,

"Could you not watch with Me for one hour?" Matthew 26:40
(NKJV)

Jesus wasn't rebuking prayerlessness alone—He was exposing the cost of absence. In the day of battle, presence matters. Prayer matters. Covering matters.

There will be Gethsemane moments in your life—seasons where the cost is heavy, the pain is real, and the decisions are eternal. And in those moments, you don't just need people who enjoy your preaching. You need people who cover your soul in prayer.

Standing in the Gap for Sons and Daughters

If you are a spiritual father, mother, pastor, or leader, you are a covering for others in their day of battle. And that responsibility is not casual—it is priestly.

Ezekiel 22:30 says, "I looked for someone among them who would build up the wall and stand before Me in the gap on behalf of the land, but I found no one." (NIV)

To cover someone is to stand in the gap. To be the reason they don't fall. To be the wall between them and destruction. To intercede when they can't. To carry their burden when they're weary. To remind them who they are when they forget.

This is the mantle of a covering: To stand in the invisible places where destinies hang in the balance.

- When your son is tempted to run—you intercede.
- When your daughter questions her calling—you speak truth.
- When the sheep come under attack—you swing the staff and drive out wolves.
- When the atmosphere is heavy—you pierce it with worship and prophetic decrees.

This is not about being dramatic—it's about being present. You're not saving people—they have their own will. But you are making war on their behalf until they remember who they are.

Covering in Crisis: The Example of Paul and Timothy

Paul knew what it meant to cover someone in battle. Timothy, his spiritual son, was timid, often unsure of himself, and ministering in an atmosphere of resistance and pressure.

In 2 Timothy 1:6–7, Paul writes:
"For this reason I remind you to fan into flame the gift of God, which is in you through the laying on of my hands. For God gave us a spirit not of fear but of power and love and self-control."
(ESV)

This was a father covering a son in the midst of fear, warfare, and temptation to retreat.

Paul wasn't just instructing Timothy—he was shielding him with words, identity, and impartation. He reminded him of his gift, his identity, and the spirit he had received.

This is how you cover sons and daughters in the day of battle:

- Remind them of who they are.
- Stir up what God put in them.
- Rebuke the lies of fear and inferiority.
- Speak with authority into their atmosphere.

Words carry power—especially when they come from a voice of spiritual authority.

How to Cover Others in Battle

If you are a covering—whether a parent, mentor, pastor, or friend—here are ways you can stand in the gap:

1. Pray Boldly and Specifically
Don't just say "God bless them." War for them. Call out

demonic assignments. Declare promises. Break confusion. Release peace.

2. Speak Identity Often
Tell them who they are, not just what they should do. Speak to their spirit, not just their behavior.

3. Discern the Battle They're In
Ask the Lord to show you what they're facing—even if they don't say it. Coverings don't wait for requests. They sense the warfare.

4. Show Up Consistently
Sometimes your presence is more powerful than your words. Be there when they're tempted to run. Stand beside them when they feel alone.

5. Remind Them They're Not Alone
The enemy wants them to feel isolated. Your covering is the evidence that God sees them, fights for them, and is not finished with them.

Conclusion: Victory Comes Through Covering

The day of battle will come. And when it does, those who are covered will stand firm. Not because they are stronger. But because they are shielded by alignment, lifted by intercession, and protected by love.

If you are a son or daughter—stay under covering. Let someone fight with you. Let someone hold up your arms. Let someone pray when you don't have words.

If you are a spiritual father or leader—cover those assigned to you. Stand in the gap. Pray in the night. Speak life in the storm. Rebuke the enemy in their atmosphere.

Victory in the Kingdom does not belong to the lone warrior. It belongs to the covered son, the covered daughter, and the house that knows how to stand together.

In the day of battle, may it be said of you:
"They were covered. And they prevailed."

Discussion Questions

1. When the day of battle comes, what difference does spiritual covering make—and how can you tell the difference between being supported and being isolated?

2. What does it practically look like to be a spiritual covering for someone else during their day of battle?

3. Why does the enemy focus so heavily on isolation—and what are the warning signs that someone is drifting out from under covering?

12

REBUILDING THE WALLS OF COVERING IN THE CHURCH

The Church in our generation is facing a crisis of covering. For too long, spiritual leaders have either abdicated their responsibility to cover others or abused their authority in ways that created deep wounds in the body. As a result, many believers today are wandering—gifted but uncovered, sincere but unaligned, passionate but disconnected.

But God is doing something in our day. There is a stirring in the Spirit to rebuild the walls of covering—to restore what was lost, to heal what was broken, and to reestablish divine order and protection in the house of God. The Lord is raising up fathers and mothers, reactivating apostolic grace, and calling His people back to covenant community where spiritual safety, correction, and alignment can be found.

In this chapter, we will explore:

- Apostolic and prophetic restoration
- Equipping spiritual fathers and mothers
- Creating a culture of covering and honor

This is more than a call to leadership reform—it is a call to return to the Kingdom blueprint for family, alignment, and spiritual authority.

The Need for Apostolic and Prophetic Restoration

The Church was never meant to function as an institution alone—it was meant to operate as a living, breathing apostolic family. Ephesians 2:20 tells us that the household of God is "built on the foundation of the apostles and prophets, with Christ Jesus Himself as the cornerstone." When those foundational gifts are absent or dishonored, the entire house becomes unstable.

In many places, pastors have been forced to carry what only apostles can establish and what only prophets can discern. As a result, the walls of spiritual protection have been compromised. Apostles build structure. Prophets reveal direction. Together, they form a spiritual wall of covering—strengthening the Church and protecting it from deception, division, and doctrinal drift.

Restoring apostolic and prophetic grace is not about returning to titles—it's about returning to function. Apostolic fathers are needed not just to build ministries, but to raise sons. Prophetic voices are needed not just to declare words, but to discern spiritual warfare, call people into alignment, and help the Church return to its first love.

Without apostolic and prophetic leadership that operates in humility and honor, the Church remains vulnerable. But when these gifts are restored—working alongside shepherds, evangelists, and teachers—we see the wall of spiritual covering rise again.

The Church as a Covenant Family, Not a Corporation

One of the primary reasons covering has been neglected in modern churches is because we've exchanged the family model for a corporate one. In the corporate model:

- Leaders are CEOs, not fathers.
- Members are employees or customers, not sons and daughters.
- Relationships are professional, not covenantal.
- Correction feels like firing, not pruning.
- Church hopping feels normal because there's no rooted family connection.

But the Church is not a business—it is a spiritual family. And in a family, covering is not optional—it's expected and it's necessary. Sons and daughters don't just come for what they can consume; they live under the wisdom, safety, and love of those called to raise them.

Rebuilding the walls of covering requires a return to the family of God—not just in theory, but in structure, leadership, and culture.

This means:

- Churches must raise fathers, not just hire staff.
- Discipleship must include correction, not just inspiration.
- Covenant must replace convenience.
- Honor must replace individualism.

Covering becomes normal again when family becomes

normal again. And when leaders lead like fathers and mothers, people begin to thrive like sons and daughters.

Equipping Spiritual Fathers and Mothers

For the walls of covering to be rebuilt, we must equip and release spiritual fathers and mothers into the Church again. This generation doesn't just need better programs—it needs people who will carry the burden of spiritual parenthood.

Paul didn't say, "You have ten thousand teachers, but not enough preachers." He said, "You have many teachers, but not many fathers." The need today is the same.

A spiritual father is someone who:

- Sees your identity and calls it out
- Covers you in correction and love
- Prays for you without needing attention
- Builds relationship over the long term
- Releases you when you are ready—not when it benefits them

A spiritual mother is someone who:

- Nurtures your calling with tenderness
- Holds your heart in confidentiality and wisdom
- Breaks shame and affirms your worth
- Protects your growth, even when it's slow
- Stands beside you when others walk away

We cannot rebuild walls of covering with only preachers and administrators. We need parents in the Spirit—those who have been healed, processed, and aligned themselves so they can now serve as a safe place for others. Training spiritual fathers and mothers will require them getting healing for their own orphan wounds.

- Teaching them healthy boundaries
- Equipping them in spiritual discernment
- Establishing them in covenant relationships
- Affirming their identity and authority

This is a call for maturity. It's time to grow up so we can raise up.

Creating a Culture of Covering and Honor

Walls are not just physical—they are cultural. The culture of a church or ministry either promotes covering or undermines it. To rebuild the walls, leaders must create a culture of honor, humility, and safety.

Here's what that culture looks like:

1. Correction Without Condemnation
People should know they can be corrected without being cut off. In a culture of covering, confrontation happens in love. The goal is restoration, not shame.

2. Honor Up, Down, and All Around
In this culture, people honor those above them (leaders), those beside them (peers), and those under their care (disciples). Honor becomes normal, not strange.

3. Vulnerability From the Top Down
Leaders model transparency. They don't pretend to be

perfect—they show how to live covered and account-able. This gives permission for others to do the same.

4. Accountability as a Blessing, Not a Burden
People don't avoid accountability—they run toward it. They understand that being seen, known, and corrected is a sign of love, not control.

5. Covenant Relationships Over Transactional Roles
Relationships are not based on performance or useful-ness, but on covenant. People stay through difficulty. Loyalty isn't blind—it's built through love.

6. Restoration Over Rejection
When someone falls, the first question is not "How could they?" but "How can we restore them?" Discipline and grace work together to rebuild lives, not discard them.

A culture of covering must be intentional. It is not built on a Sunday sermon—it is built through ongoing relationships, prayer, structure, and consistent modeling of godly leadership.

Building Churches That Cover the City

God's desire is not just to build churches that gather—He wants to raise houses that cover. A church that functions as a spiritual covering will not only protect its people—it will cover its city. It becomes a spiritual gate, a place of refuge, and a wall of intercession for its region.

When a church walks in proper covering:

- Demonic strongholds are pushed back

- Families are healed and restored
- Sons and daughters are launched into destiny
- Cities begin to feel the weight of the Kingdom

The Church becomes a governmental people, not just a gathering of believers. It walks in apostolic authority because it lives under divine order. It becomes a lighthouse, not just a sanctuary.

To build this kind of house, leaders must:

- Reestablish spiritual fathering
- Teach and model submission and honor
- Confront control and spiritual abuse
- Heal past wounds through inner healing and deliverance
- Prioritize presence over performance
- Build teams that walk in alignment, not ambition

The rebuilding process won't be easy. But it is essential. Nehemiah didn't rebuild the walls of Jerusalem with professional builders—he used families. The same is true today. It takes spiritual family to rebuild spiritual walls.

The Final Picture: A Church in Divine Order

What does a Church look like where the walls of covering have been restored?

1. It is a place where leaders are known as fathers and mothers, not just bosses or figureheads.
2. It is a place where sons and daughters are not afraid to be seen, corrected, and loved.

3. It is a place where the gifts of the Spirit flow freely, under order and accountability.
4. It is a place where honor is the atmosphere, not competition.
5. It is a place where intercession protects the house and launches destinies.
6. It is a place where restoration is the norm and shame has no home.
7. It is a place where people know, without a doubt: "I am covered here."

This is the kind of Church Jesus is returning for—a glorious bride, without spot or wrinkle, walking in unity, purity, and power.

And it begins when we rebuild the walls.

Conclusion: Rise and Build

The Spirit is saying in this hour what He said to Nehemiah and his generation:

"You see the trouble we are in... Come, let us rebuild the wall... and we will no longer be in disgrace." (Nehemiah 2:17 NIV)

The disgrace of disconnection, division, abuse, and spiritual orphanhood is being broken. God is raising a people who will not only come under covering, but who will rise up to become pillars, fathers, mothers, and spiritual protectors. The question is no longer whether the walls are broken—it's whether we will rise and build.

Let the call go forth.
Let the fathers return.

Let the sons arise.

Let the walls of covering be rebuilt—for this generation and the next.

Discussion Questions

1 . In what ways have we seen the Church operate more like a corporation than a covenant family—and how has that shift impacted our ability to walk in spiritual covering?

2 . Why is the restoration of apostolic and prophetic leadership critical to rebuilding spiritual covering in the Church today?

3 . What qualities make a spiritual father or mother trustworthy—and what steps can we take to grow into that kind of leader for the next generation?

CONCLUSION
LIVING COVERED AND BECOMING A
SHELTER FOR OTHERS

This book has taken us on a journey—a journey from Eden to the early Church, from spiritual orphans to empowered sons, from isolation to alignment, from wandering to covering. We've looked at the principle, the function, the call, and the danger surrounding spiritual covering. Now, we arrive at the final question:

Will you live covered—and become a shelter for others?

In a world fractured by distrust, spiritual abuse, and father-lessness, this is not just a nice idea—it is a Kingdom imperative. If we are going to see revival that remains, if we are going to build churches that last, if we are going to launch sons and daughters into destiny, we must not only come under covering —we must become coverings.

This final conclusion is a call to action. A call to legacy. A call to take everything you've received in these pages and build a spiritual house that covers others.

The Legacy of Covering

Covering is not just about protection in your present—it's about legacy in the future. Every time you walk in alignment, stay submitted, receive correction, or pray for your covering, you are building something that your children and spiritual descendants will walk in.

Legacy doesn't begin with platforms—it begins with posture.

Think of the great legacies of faith throughout Scripture. Abraham's obedience, Moses' intercession, David's worship, Paul's spiritual fathering—they all lived under God's covering, and each became a conduit of that covering to those who followed them.

You don't have to be famous to leave a legacy. You just have to be faithful. If you stay covered, those under you will learn to live covered. And when storms come, they won't be scattered—they'll be shielded.

This generation needs more than inspiration. It needs impartation. It needs people who have been processed, protected, pruned, and promoted—not by self, but by submission.

When you live covered, you're not just avoiding disaster. You're building a generational wall of protection. Your children will inherit spiritual order, not confusion. Your disciples will be launched, not lost. Your ministry will have longevity, not just momentum.

Covering is not just about you. It's about who's coming after you.

Building Houses That Cover

God is not just raising up individuals—He's raising up houses. Spiritual families. Apostolic centers. Churches that function not just as gatherings, but as shelters. Places where:

- The lost are found
- The broken are healed
- The orphaned become sons
- The gifted are aligned
- The anointed are accountable
- The mature are multiplied

We need houses that cover—not control. Houses that protect, not police. Houses where the gifts of the Spirit can flow under godly authority, not chaos. Houses that build up people, not just programs. Houses where fathers and mothers are raised, not just administrators and volunteers.

To build such a house, three essential pillars must be in place:

1. Alignment at the Top
The leadership must be covered. Pastors must be submitted. Apostles must be in relationship. There must be no lone wolves at the helm. The house cannot cover what the head refuses to submit to.

2. A Culture of Honor
Honor must flow up, down, and across. Correction is not seen as rejection, and accountability is not seen as control. In a culture of honor, people grow without fear. Truth is spoken in love. Trust is guarded. Gossip is

crushed. And everyone knows their role in the family matters.

3. Structures That Serve Sons, Not Systems
The systems of the house must serve the purpose of raising sons and daughters—not just running programs. Ministries exist to disciple people, not impress people. The success of the house is not in how many attend but in how many are transformed, aligned, and sent.

When a house is built with these pillars, it becomes a refuge in the storm, a beacon in the city, a womb for revival, and a resting place for the glory of God.

God's Design for Safety in Spiritual Family

Covering is not a man-made idea—it is God's design. It was in Eden. It was in the tabernacle. It was in the blood of the Lamb over the doorposts in Egypt. It was in the relationship of Jesus and His Father. It was in Paul and Timothy. It was in the early Church. And it is in the blueprint of the Church today.

God designed His people to live in spiritual family.

The Psalmist writes, "God sets the solitary in families" (Psalm 68:6). That is not just a relational statement—it is a protective one. Family is God's idea for safety, identity, and legacy.

In a spiritual family:

- You are seen even when you're not on stage.
- You are known even when you're struggling.
- You are corrected even when you don't want to be.

- You are protected even when you don't feel the danger.
- You are launched when you're ready—and sometimes when you don't feel ready, but God knows it's time.

The safest place to be in spiritual warfare is not just under a roof—it's in a family with covering.

Becoming a Shelter for Others

This book began with the question: Who covers you? But we now arrive at the greater question: Who are you called to cover? Once you've been covered, healed, aligned, and released —it's time to turn around and build a shelter for someone else.

This is how Kingdom legacy works. You don't graduate from covering—you multiply it. You don't move on from being a son —you become a father. You don't just survive the storm—you build a house others can hide in.

Here's how you become a shelter:

- Stay covered yourself—never outgrow alignment.
- Let God process your pain so you don't pass it on.
- Create safe spaces where others can be vulnerable.
- Speak life over sons and daughters.
- Be consistent—don't abandon those under your care.
- Fight in the spirit for those too weary to war.
- Release people into their calling without control.

When you become a shelter, you become a representation of the Father's heart. You become the voice someone else needed. You become the one who says, "You don't have to run. You can rest here."

The End Is the Beginning

As we come to the end of this book, remember this truth: Being covered is not a one-time decision. It is a lifestyle. A posture. A covenant. A calling.

You may shift assignments. You may grow in leadership. You may gain influence. But you never outgrow the need for covering. You never graduate from sonship. You never stop needing spiritual family.

The greatest leaders in Scripture were those who stayed aligned:

- Jesus always honored the Father's voice.
- David refused to touch Saul until God removed him.
- Elisha refused to leave Elijah's side until the mantle fell.
- Timothy remained a son, even as he became a leader.

These were not weak men—they were covered men. And because they were covered, they carried weight, walked in power, and left legacy.

A Final Charge

If you've walked through these chapters and felt conviction —good. That's the Spirit calling you deeper.

- If you've seen yourself as the uncovered one—it's time to return.
- If you've seen yourself as the one called to cover—it's time to rise.
- If you've been hurt by covering—it's time to heal.
- If you've led with control—it's time to repent.
- If you've been afraid of alignment—it's time to trust again.

The Church cannot function without covering. Sons cannot grow without fathers. Cities cannot be transformed without houses that are aligned and accountable. The walls must be rebuilt—and you are part of the plan.

Let It Be Said of You...

Let it be said that you were covered in the day of battle.

Let it be said that you carried sons and daughters with joy.

Let it be said that your house was a shelter from the storm.

Let it be said that you raised up others, not for your glory, but for theirs.

Let it be said that you walked in humility, authority, and alignment.

Let it be said that you lived covered—and became a place of covering.

Because in the end, when the war is over and the dust

settles, the Father will look for one thing: "Did you carry My heart?" And if you did—you carried covering.

Now go. Build. Cover. Restore. And become the shelter God designed you to be. The world is waiting. The Church is groaning. The sons are crying. Who will cover them?

Let the answer be: I will.

ABOUT THE AUTHOR

Tom Cornell is the Senior Leader of SOZO Church in Washington state, founder of Walk in the Light International and SOZO Network. Tom is married to his beautiful wife Katy and lives in the Puget Sound area with her and their three kids. He has been in ministry pastoring and teaching the body of Christ since 2008.

He has a passion to see the body of Christ moving from people with an orphan mindset to that of sonship; equipping the body to do the work of Jesus resulting in seeing the Kingdom of God manifested here on earth.

www.ingramcontent.com/pod-product-compliance
Lightning Source LLC
Chambersburg PA
CBHW071226090426
42736CB00014B/2989